ADVANCE PRAISE

What a story! Your "normal" might not look exactly like Jeff's, but I know it's going to contain some things you weren't expecting. Jeff's tale of how he rebuilt his life will give you the courage to weather the storms you face, too.

—**JON ACUFF**, Author of *Finish: Give Yourself the Gift of Done*

Normal is something many of us try to find. But God often reveals that his path of disruption is far more beautiful than our plan of normal. Jeff's story is very clear proof of that. I highly recommend this book.

—**JEREMY COWART**, Photographer & Founder of The Purpose Hotel

About a year ago, I first sat down with Jeff and he shared his amazing story. I was so moved that I changed my plans that weekend and invited Jeff to share it with our whole church. People still talk about that unforgettable day. Finding Normal *captures this powerful and compelling story. Read this book . . . the pages are filled with honest, raw, and hope-filled redemption.*

—**DARREN WHITEHEAD**, Founder & Lead Pastor at Church of the City, Franklin, TN

Finding Normal *is Jeff and his family's open and honest story of their journey—one full of heartbreak yet hope. I have personally seen Jeff and Jacqui rely on their faith through times of immense trial. I can't imagine "finding normal" when everything you once knew is suddenly different. I am honored to know them and inspired by how they are living out their faith and sharing their story.*

—**TASHA LAYTON**, Pastor, Teacher, & Worship Leader

Jeff and his remarkable story are a bold reminder that we can use what makes us weird to make our world more wonderful.

—**CJ CASCIOTTA**, Author & Media Maker

I know Jeff's book will inspire and encourage everyone who reads it. His story is life changing and I am blessed to call him a close friend.

—**JACK VALE**, Comedian & Producer

Jeff's story is sobering and thought-provoking. I'm reminded that nothing in this life is within our control, no matter how in control we feel, and nothing in life is outside of God's plan, no matter how alone or aimless we believe ourselves to be. Jeff's story is a testimony of the beauty made only through trials and tragedy. You'll be challenged to live life to the fullest and use every breath for God's glory! A must read for sure!

—**KEITH SMITH**, Producer & Member of TobyMac's DiverseCity Band

In Finding Normal, *Jeff shares his amazing story in such a vulnerable and powerful way. This book clearly presents a beautiful picture of hope and restoration for all who will read it.*

—**CURTIS ZACKERY**, Pastor & Author of *Soul Rest: Reclaim Your Life, Return to Sabbath*

Coming from someone who has personally dealt with a near fatal injury, making permanent new challenges and new realities, I guarantee Jeff's story will encourage you on your journey to finding a new normal.

—**AARON "CANON" MCCAIN**, Hip-Hop Artist

Wow! There is only one response to be had after reading this book and that is to worship God our Father because of His glory and immense goodness. Jeff's story is not only one of personal tragedy and triumph; it is also one that paints a beautiful picture of God's sovereignty over our circumstances. We believe every reader's faith will be deepened through Jeff's amazing story. May we all be strengthened by this book to place our hope in Jesus through every change and every challenge.

—**KELLIE & KRISTEN**, Worship Leaders & Songwriters

This book will challenge you, uplift you and inspire you. Jeff's story is one that needs to be heard. Read this book.

—**JASON ROMANO,** Author of *Live to Forgive* & Host of the Sports Spectrum Podcast

Jeff's story is both sobering and inspiring. It is a reminder to hold all that we have with open hands, trusting that the Lord's plans are better than our own. It is a story of loss but, ultimately, of redemption and victory, and it is sure to leave you feeling challenged and encouraged. Finding Normal is a must-read!

—**BECCA BRADLEY**, Christian Singer, Songwriter, & Multi-Instrumentalist

Finding Normal

finding ing nor mal

An Uninvited
Change, An
Unexpected
Outcome

Jeff Huxford, M.D.

NASHVILLE

LONDON • NEW YORK • MELBOURNE • VANCOUVER

Finding Normal

An Uninvited Change, An Unexpected Outcome

Published in New York, New York, by Morgan James Publishing. Morgan James is a trademark of Morgan James, LLC. www.MorganJamesPublishing.com

The Morgan James Speakers Group can bring authors to your live event. For more information or to book an event visit The Morgan James Speakers Group at www.TheMorganJamesSpeakersGroup.com.

ISBN 9781683509301 paperback
ISBN 9781683509318 eBook
Library of Congress Control Number: 2018930672

Cover Design by:
Micah Kandros Design

Interior Design by:
Chris Treccani
www.3dogcreative.net

In an effort to support local communities, raise awareness and funds, Morgan James Publishing donates a percentage of all book sales for the life of each book to Habitat for Humanity Peninsula and Greater Williamsburg.

Get involved today! Visit
www.MorganJamesBuilds.com

To my loving and faithful wife, Jacqui, and two amazing children, Jayse and Jenna. I love you with everything I have and will ever be. Thank you for always loving me and your never-ending support of my "new normal." I know this story isn't just mine. It belongs to all of us!

TABLE OF CONTENTS

———

FOREWORD

———

Tragedy has a way of changing the way we view our lives. Not just physically or mentally, but also spiritually. It forces us to evaluate what's important in life. It makes us take a step back and analyze everything we've ever done, said, and wished we would have said and done. In the blink of an eye our lives could change for the worse, the better, or for the same. But the real question isn't what might happen, but how are we going to respond to these tragedies when they do occur.

It's easy to go about our lives trusting God when things are going our way. But what about when they don't? What happens when everything we thought we knew and understood changes? What happens when the life we have is completely flipped upside down? What will our relationship with God look like then? That's the real question. All throughout the Bible we see people faced with tragedy and despair. Some of them turn away from God, while some of them lean in closer to him. Tragedy is inevitable, but the way we respond to it is up to us. Jeff's story is a beautiful example of tragedy, which ultimately ends in triumph.

All throughout my life I've seen tragedy and pain change people, including myself. Some for the better. Some for worse. Some found peace. Others found continuous heartbreak and rejection. But regardless of what one may feel or experience, we cannot forget what the Bible says about God amidst these times; he's always with us (Deut. 31:6). He never leaves us. He's always guiding us, directing us, correcting us, and encouraging us toward a life that moves us closer to him. The Bible tells us to come to Jesus when we are weary and heavy burdened, for he will give us rest. You will see Jeff doing that throughout the pages of this compelling book.

We have to understand that sometimes life just happens, things change, tragedy occurs, and our plans might not always go the way we thought they would. This doesn't mean that God is absent or unloving; it means that sometimes there is nothing we can do about it except trust him for wisdom and guidance along the way, even when no victory or end is in sight. We must learn to trust God in the midst of tragedy, learn to embrace uncertainty, and follow the voice of God. It's a voice that always lead us to the path of *finding normal*.

Jeff's book is sure to inspire and encourage anyone who has been through or is currently enduring a difficult season in their life.

– **JARRID WILSON**, Pastor, Author of *Love Is Oxygen*, and Founder of Anthem of Hope

PREFACE

---

normal: conforming to a standard;
usual, typical, or expected

As you begin to read this book, it won't take long for you to figure out that I think about "normal" a lot! Specifically, I have considered what that word means for me and my life. Now, this all started when my doctors repeatedly brought up how traumatic brain injury (TBI) patients must find a "new normal" after suffering a brain injury. When I set out to find mine, I really had no idea what I was doing, but I ended up finding something I wasn't expecting. And what I discovered had a profound and lasting effect on my life. It changed everything about me.

In my search for a new normal, I realized "normal" is a reasonable adjective to use when describing an inanimate object, but a worthless descriptor of people, because when it comes to us humans, it doesn't exist. There's really no such thing. Despite the fact that it's impossible, "you should just try to be more normal" is something that's still encouraged in our society. But I have learned it's not only impossible; it's also undesirable. At least, undesirable in the way our society defines it and how I used to see it.

INTRODUCTION

———

I know it's impossible to predict a patient's future, but by studying outcomes of patients with similar illnesses or injuries, doctors can make predictions based on the information they gather. Based on the severity of my brain injury, doctors are unsure how much longer I will be able to do what I am currently doing, but one report reads "an optimistic estimate is five to ten years." (*Note: At the time I'm writing this book, it's been five years since my accident.*)

This is certainly a scary thought, but I'm trying not to let fear control me. I'm also not going to take any chances. I want my family, friends, and others to remember who I am, and more importantly, "whose" I am, long after I can no longer tell them. That's why I decided to write this book sooner rather than later.

*****

All of us will undoubtedly face trials during our lifetimes. Tough times will occur that we can never truly prepare for, nor do we usually try, because we all assume "something like that could never happen to me." But such times are inevitable. And when they happen, we can choose to deny their existence, but this can only last for so long. Sooner or later we have to face them head on. When admitting and confronting them, we must try our best to move forward in spite of whatever lies in front of us. This is typically a case of learning as we go, because even though someone may have gone through something similar, each individual experience is unique. We reluctantly receive what I would call an "on-the-job training experience."

These trials may not always make sense. We will often fail to find any reason for them. They will rarely be convenient and will often be uncomfortable. But I've realized that anything can be used and redeemed by God if we hand it over to him. I can't say this has always been my perspective or characterized my approach to difficult situations in the past, nor have I yet perfected the practice of self-surrender. I often still want and try to take care of things myself. But I'm coming to realize the importance and the beauty of relinquishing everything to God, the good and the bad, the expected and the unexpected, even when I don't know what lies ahead, what tomorrow may bring, or what the future may hold.

Charles Spurgeon once said, *"The Lord's mercy often rides to the door of our heart upon the black horse of affliction."[1]* He couldn't have been more right. Sometimes it takes a seemingly impossible situation so we'll begin turning our hearts and souls fully to God.

---

1   C.H. Spurgeon, *All of Grace* (CreateSpace Independent Publishing Platform, 2013).

CHAPTER 1

Re-living Normal

Normal Beginnings

I believe in order to appreciate someone's story and where they are currently, it's important to know where they came from. So let me tell you about where I came from, or who I was before my accident, the accident that changed everything about me and when my life got a restart. This story isn't easy to tell, but it's necessary because I want others to know they're not alone. They're not the only ones who have questioned what God was doing in their lives, nor are they the only ones who questioned if God truly knew what was best for them.

I grew up in a typical middle-class family in rural Indiana. I was raised by two loving parents. I had one older brother and lived close to all my extended family. I was raised on a large family farm and started working on it at a young age. This taught me the importance of hard work and responsibility. I took all that I had learned on the farm with me for the rest of my life. It helped mold and shape me into the man I would become through the years. Growing up, I was always a good student and took my education seriously. Sports was also an integral part of my youth. But most importantly, I was born and raised in the church, and God was always an important part of my life. This foundation prepared me for what I would face in my future and, but for this foundation, I'm not sure where I would be today.

Although I made plenty of mistakes along the way, which all of us do, God was an integral part of who I was and who I became. It reminds me of the story found in *Matthew 7* where Jesus is explaining the difference between a life built on the rock as opposed to one built upon the shifting sand. We know that the rock is just another illustration for building upon the foundational promises of Jesus, with the sand representing anything other than him. God, our rock, is the only immoveable foundation that we can rely on to keep us safe, secure, and focused on what really matters in the world.

Therefore, everyone who hears these words of mine and acts on them will be like a wise man who built his house on the rock. The rain fell, the rivers rose, and the winds blew and pounded that house. Yet it didn't collapse, because its foundation was on the rock. But everyone who hears these words of mine and doesn't act on them will be like a foolish man who built his house on the sand. The rain fell, the rivers rose, the winds blew and pounded that house, and it collapsed. It collapsed with a great crash. (Matt. 7:24–27, NIV)

You see, for as long as I can remember, I have always believed in God and considered him to be an important part of my life. I tried to put him at the forefront of everything I did. It was part of who our family was and what we represented. This was one of the reasons that I, at a fairly young age, accepted Jesus as my Lord and Savior, publicly proclaimed my faith, and was baptized.

I recall going to church on most Sundays and following all the rules needed to maintain the reputation of a "good" Christian, which I believe is very similar to most of American Christianity today. This rules-and-checklist mindset led to a self-centered faith, and because of that I never totally surrendered my life to God. I still counted on myself to do the bulk of the "work" and grossly overestimated my contribution to my salvation. But I'm extremely thankful that I've come to realize the truth. That my relationship and standing with God has nothing to do with me and has everything to do with the one in whose hands I put my life.

A lot of what I did and how I lived out my faith when I was younger was motivated by selfish pride. I wanted to use Jesus to improve my own status and to get what I wanted. I had no intention of using my life to glorify and point others to him. I was doing "good" things, not doing "bad" things, and living an overall moral life, but it was never really about Jesus. It was about me and mine, my image, my family's image. Pride controlled me, but I had it masked as humility and hard work.

I'm not ungrateful for being raised in a Christian home, and my foundation wasn't completely false and cracked. I just realize some things now that I didn't realize back then. I am very thankful for the way I was brought up. In fact, it's a huge reason for the way I am today. My upbringing in the church helped build my character and strengthen my moral fabric. Even though I was often unclear why I was doing the things I was doing, who I should be doing it for, and where the power for doing those things came from, it kept me headed in the right direction and on the right path.

The College Years: A Brief and Slight Detour

I never stopped believing in Jesus, not even close. Nor did I start going down the wrong path in the obvious ways. I wasn't partying, getting drunk, doing drugs, or sleeping around. I remained a "moral" individual. I was actually a "wanted man" on campus because I could always be counted on as the designated driver. But I didn't mind being known for this because I had many great friends and others around campus who respected me for who I was and what I stood for. *(Believe it or not, I was highly respected for my sweet dance moves! Don't laugh!)*

While my faith in God didn't necessarily disappear when I was in college, it also didn't grow. I was stagnant. And if you know anything about stagnant water, you know it's prone to filth and disease. There is nothing in this world that's stagnant and good. The two words oppose each other on so many levels.

During these years I didn't give much thought to church or my faith. I guess I figured nobody has time for Jesus during their college years. At least, that's how I saw it. It led to the lukewarm type of faith God talks so harshly and bluntly about in Revelation.

"So, because you are lukewarm—neither hot nor cold—I am about to spit you out of my mouth." (Rev. 3:16, NIV)

So many of us are focused on finding ourselves during college that we fail to realize how important God can be in our lives. But because everyone else I knew was following suit, I figured that my lukewarm faith and the resultant lifestyle must be considered an *excused absence*. I was just pressing pause and joining in with the rest of the crowd. With my busy class schedule and my skewed view of what it meant to be a Christian, I assumed all of this was perfectly acceptable to Jesus and a completely normal way for a college student to act.

I guess when you don't have any accountability as it pertains to your faith, that type of thing can happen. I realize how important accountability and faith-based community is now, but back then it was the last thing on my mind. I didn't see community as necessary. The pastors and faith-based leaders who, over the years, ran into trouble because of immorality could all have been saved if they'd put accountability and guardrails in place. Accountability really does matter, and I wish I would have had more of it when I was in college. I wonder what my life would look like today if I had lived out my faith in a real and tangible way rather than keeping it in the backseat and ignoring it back in those days. Would things be different? I don't know, and I can't dwell on those questions. But I can certainly encourage people not to make the same mistakes I did and instead encourage them to put their relationship with God at the forefront of their life.

You'll never regret living life with accountability, focused on glorifying God and being passionate about exuding the love of God to those around you. But a life without these things is a different story.

Getting Back on the Right Track (Kind of)

After graduating from college, I moved to Indianapolis and began attending medical school. During this time I started going to a church that was unlike any I had been to before. This church was what, I guess, you could call "contemporary," and most of the people there were close to my age. I started attending this church regularly and even joined a community group, a group of like-minded believers with whom I could journey in faith. During this time I realized I had been missing the complete picture of who Jesus is and the fullness of his gospel. This church changed a lot about me. I still wasn't perfect by any stretch of the word, but I was making progress. This church showed me what faith in Jesus is supposed to look like. It showed me what it meant to be a true, authentic follower of Jesus.

I didn't realize it at the time, but my faith was still being driven by selfish intent. A lot of what I was doing was to better myself and my image. I was pretty self-centered. I wanted Jesus because of what he could give me; it never crossed my mind that I could do something for him. Even though my faith was growing deeper, I was still elevating the idea of becoming a successful doctor, and my own personal achievements and goals were my main focuses.

I graduated from medical school and was now officially a medical doctor, something I had dreamed of being for many years. I married my wife, Jacqui, and we moved to Bristol, Tennessee, where I began a three-year family practice residency. Life was progressing well and according to plan. I was achieving everything I had ever hoped for. We joined a local church in Tennessee and became highly involved in the youth ministry. On top of spending a great amount of time with the students, I was also playing guitar and leading worship at the church's Wednesday night service.

Man, I remember feeling pretty good about myself at the time. Here I was, able to carve out time for church and Jesus, even while working the busy schedule of a resident physician. I felt worthy of some special recognition! I am not trying to downplay the importance of what I did during those years, because I think God still used them for a lot of good. But much of what I was doing was motivated by selfish desires and I wanted to impress people with my commitment to my faith in spite of my busy schedule. If I was able to find the time and energy to do all I was doing for the church, then I didn't want to hear their excuses for their inactivity.

The Start of My American Dream

After finishing my residency, Jacqui, our then 4 month old son, Jayse, and I moved back to my wife's hometown of DeMotte, Indiana, where I started my career as a family doctor. After many years of schooling and residency, I was finally doing what I'd always wanted to do and something I felt I was pretty good at. I was proud to be a doctor and was passionate about helping my patients.

We immediately got involved in the church my wife grew up in. I started playing guitar in the praise band, and my wife and I jumped right in as small-group leaders. We were excited to begin pouring into others. It seemed like everything was going very well in my spiritual life and things were all falling into place. Not only that, but I was really starting to find my groove as a small-town family "Doc." I was thriving at my job and quickly building a sizable, loyal patient base. People respected me for who I was and I was earning the trust of the community we lived in.

I was accomplishing everything I had always dreamed of. The job, the wife, the kids, the house, all of it. Things were going incredibly well from the outside looking in. And I always made sure to, at least, include Jesus in everything I was doing and trying to accomplish. He was more than welcome to be a part of my life. I just wasn't ready to give him total control of it.

Here's the truth of the matter. I wasn't chasing the real Jesus. There are many things in this world that constantly pull and beg for our attention, our heart, our worship, and our soul. The battle for our heart that takes place every day is active and begs to be acknowledged if one seeks any chance of keeping themselves on a straight and narrow path. Why? Because if we don't learn to put up our guard as Christians, the enemy will seek every opportunity he can to steal, kill, and destroy our hearts (John 10:10).

When we pursue after the hope of Jesus, we are pursuing life to the fullest extent—the only true experience of life that really exists. But when we pursue after anything contrary to that of God's Word, we set ourselves up for failure. Don't be tricked into thinking that the temptations of this world can offer anything remotely close to the fulfillment and peace of Jesus. They can't, and they never will be able to live up to what God has designed for humanity.

Movies, music, advertisements, fame, materialism, money, billboards, magazines, social media. All of these things, although not always bad, can tempt and persuade you to chase after something other than Christ. Sometimes the temptation is obvious, but other times it may seem justified. Regardless of what or who is tempting you, the reality and importance of needing to guard our hearts remain the same. If we're not chasing Jesus, we are chasing a lie. Let us choose to pick up our crosses daily, pursue after the hope of Jesus, and dedicate our lives to making much of him and nothing of ourselves.

Pride Issues

Pride was always an issue for me. I wasn't an outright arrogant person, but in my unseen depths I was very pleased with myself for how "good" I was doing, and because of this I felt I deserved everything good that came my way. I know many of us deal with the inner battle of pride, and it's something that can really mess with you if not corrected. God warns of this in the book of Proverbs.

> *Get wisdom—it's worth more than money; choose insight over income every time. The road of right living bypasses evil; watch your step and save your life. First pride, then the crash—the bigger the ego, the harder the fall. It's better to live humbly among the poor than to live it up among the rich and famous. It pays to take life seriously; things work out when you trust in God. (Prov. 16:17–20, MSG)*

We have to understand being a Christian means that all we do, accomplish, and achieve is because of him and for his glory. It's no longer about us and our own platforms. Christianity requires nothing of us and everything of Christ. It's the essence of true humility. Looking back, I realize how much humility I lacked even though I portrayed myself as someone who had it. It's crazy what we trick ourselves into believing so we can then justify our unwillingness to change. We lie to ourselves so we feel better about the overall situation. I know I'm not the first one who has struggled with this and I, for certain, won't be the last. It's a daily battle we all face. The flesh yearns for something different than the love of Christ, and we must stand guard to avoid pursuing a life that gratifies self instead of Savior. The Bible shows us the results of pride through the example of King Nebuchadnezzar. He became prideful and consequently was humbled by God's power and truth.

Daniel 5:20–21 (NIV) says,

But when Nebuchadnezzar's heart became arrogant and hardened with pride, he was deposed from his royal throne and stripped of his glory. He was driven away from people and given the mind of an animal; he lived with the wild donkeys and ate grass like cattle; and his body was drenched with the dew of heaven, until he acknowledged that the Most High God is sovereign over the kingdoms of men and sets over them anyone he wishes.

King Nebuchadnezzar lived like an animal until he came to his senses and repented. God forgave him, saw that he had pure motives, and restored the kingdom to him. It was only after he let go of his pride that God truly blessed him. God had no time for the king's arrogance and pride, and the same is true with us.

Another example is King Herod in Acts 12:20–24 (MSG):

But things went from bad to worse for Herod. Now people from Tyre and Sidon put him on the warpath. But they got Blastus, King Herod's right-hand man, to put in a good word for them and got a delegation together to iron things out. Because they were dependent on Judea for food supplies, they couldn't afford to let this go on too long. On the day set for their meeting, Herod, robed in pomposity, took his place on the throne and regaled them with a lot of hot air. The people played their part to the hilt and shouted flatteries: "The voice of God! The voice of God!"

That was the last straw. God had had enough of Herod's arrogance and sent an angel to strike him down. Herod had given God no credit for anything. Down he went. Rotten to the core, a maggoty old man if there ever was one, he died. Meanwhile, the ministry of God's Word grew by leaps and bounds.

Things escalated quickly and Herod was eaten by worms and died. This is a pretty crazy story, but I believe God went to the extreme in this case to show how much he despises people who have prideful hearts, especially those who try to take credit from him.

We can use the examples of Nebuchadnezzar and Herod as reminders of what will happen when we begin thinking too much of ourselves and doing things in hopes of gaining attention and praise. God doesn't have anything against people being praised for the good things they do, just as long as they don't allow those praises to be their foundation and worth. Not to mention, they should also make sure they are redirecting the praise and glory back to the person who deserves it in the first place.

They say pride comes before a fall. The second a man thinks he has things under control is the moment when everything can collapse in the blink of an eye. That is why we must make sure we keep ourselves in check, as pride is the last thing we want infiltrating our hearts.

Losing the American Dream

"Our greatest fear should not be of failure but of succeeding at things in life that don't really matter."[2]
—FRANCIS CHAN

The American dream had almost been guaranteed to me if I followed a certain set of guidelines. And to this point it had proven to be a legitimate guarantee. From the outside looking in, mine was the story of a normal American kid raised by a normal family in a normal home. I went on to earn my medical degree and became a family physician. It was one version of what every American strives for.

But when the so-called American Dream was taken from me, it didn't take long to realize this wasn't the dream I should have been seeking. My tragedy had a way of awakening my spirit to what was really important in life. The dream I should have been after could not be reached by any work I could do, but only by resting in the work already done by someone.

---

2   Francis Chan and Danae Yankoski, *Crazy Love: Overwhelmed by a Relentless God* (Colorado Springs: David C. Cook, 2013).

Someone I already knew a lot *about* but had never fully *known*. His name was Jesus.

Normally, when people come face to face with their pride, it's because of a traumatic event that caused them to rethink everything about themselves, who they are, and why they're on this earth. That's exactly what happened to me. Just when I thought I had it all together, something took place that stripped it all away. And while I'm not going to say that God caused it to happen, I will say that he used it to wake me up spiritually, to re-prioritize my life, and to realize what's really important.

CHAPTER 2

Losing Normal

Dear TBI,
My doctors are unsure how I am doing what I am
doing today when they see the damage you did
to my brain. There is a lot of speculation over
how much longer I will even have the ability to
function. It's not going to be easy, but I'm going
to try and ignore this ominous forecast. I want
to stay living in the moment and not give much
thought to what you could bring me in the future.
—JEFF

Nothing

Heaven is for Real. Miracles from Heaven. 90 Minutes in Heaven. These are just a few of the many books written and movies made about people's near-death experiences. They're all well written, and regardless of their theological foundations, the stories themselves are amazing and thought-provoking. Many of these books have a similar story. They tell about how someone went to heaven and met God after a tragic event; God then explains he wasn't ready for them yet so he sends them back here to Earth to complete their mission. Each author goes into detail about what God and heaven looked like, whom they saw while they were there, and other various illustrations.

Given my longing to add some flair to my somewhat boring life story, I wish I could tell you something along those lines about the day I almost died, but I can't. I don't remember anything about what happened at the scene of the accident and what I was experiencing while I was there. In fact, this nothingness lasted for quite a while. I may have been "awake" for the first couple weeks after my accident, but I wasn't really there. I was just existing, not really living or interacting with my environment. The first thing I remember is waking up and thinking I was on vacation. I looked out my hotel room and saw what I thought was the ocean, but it was actually downtown Chicago and I was in a tenth-floor hospital room overlooking Lake Michigan.

I typically have no problem recalling important events from my past. I can remember places I have been, the people I was with, and most of what was taking place around me. Sometimes I can remember minute, often meaningless, details about such occasions. What sometimes stands out the most about these occasions is the emotions associated with them: joy, sadness, excitement, fear, etc. But most of these events did not alter the course of my life and the emotions they elicited were only temporary. It doesn't make any sense that I am unable to remember what happened or the emotions I was feeling on the day I suffered my brain injury, a day that changed me in such a profound and permanent way.

The Day Everything Changed

Everything is going your way. You're living the dream. You have a loving spouse, wonderful children, great friends, and a rewarding career. You're doing what everyone else wishes they could do. Then tragedy strikes unexpectedly and you nearly lose it all, everything, even your very life. Doctors are telling your loved ones—not you because you are in a semi-comatose state—that they aren't sure what to expect next. They aren't sure you'll survive, and if you do, they aren't sure how much function you'll regain. I was a successful family practice doctor, and it appeared I had everything a guy could really ask for: a great job, a beautiful and supportive wife, and two wonderful and healthy kids. That's what happened to me, and I literally never saw it coming.

It was May 3, 2012. This was the day my new life began and my new story started. It started out like any other day off. It was a Thursday, and I had run into town to purchase a few things for our house while my son was in school and my wife and daughter were manning the garage sale we were having at our home. The last thing I remember was being in the hardware store, taking pictures of a few items, texting them to my wife, Jacqui, and asking whether or not she wanted me to buy them. This is the point where everything goes black, where everything goes fuzzy and disappears.

You never really picture yourself getting into a near-fatal, life-changing accident, so it's not usually something you would ever try to prepare yourself for. Why would you want to? It's one of those things you say "will never happen to me," regardless of how many times you have seen it happen to others. It's not that I always thought myself above it but just that it wasn't in the cards for my life. It wasn't what God had planned for my life. But I guess you never know what's going to happen in the future, and all you can really do to prepare yourself is to have faith and trust in God that everything is going to be okay, even when it doesn't feel like it.

*****

I don't remember leaving the store or what happened the rest of the day. But I have been told many stories and seen numerous pictures of it, so I was able to create a mental picture of the rest of the day's events. I pulled up to one of our town's busiest intersections, a red flashing light at a four-way stop on a highway. Normally, everybody stops and waits at the light, driving through when it's their turn. When it was mine and I proceeded to make my way into the intersection, a large work truck blew through a red light, hitting the passenger side of my truck and pinning it up against a large concrete pole, where my head smashed through the driver's side window, then striking the pole with tremendous force.

Based on how the accident scene appeared, everyone who passed by and witnessed its aftermath figured the driver of my truck was dead. They believed there was no way someone could escape from that type of accident alive.

I know that because of the severity of my accident and the extent of the damage to my truck, I really shouldn't be here today. It doesn't make any sense that I survived the accident and am alive to tell you this story. But I am. And that's why I believe my story needs to be shared.

Did I Say Something About a "Testimony"?

I don't remember it that clearly, but my wife remembers something I said just prior to my accident that foreshadowed what would soon take place in my life—our lives.

One night, everyone was sharing their testimonies at a small group that met at our house every week. It's something we did sometimes, especially when someone new joined the group. When it was my turn to share, I expressed frustration to the group about my lack of a powerful story. I was complaining that my testimony wasn't filled with enough struggles, trials, and tribulation. Because of this, I felt my story was too boring.

You see, I had been born and raised in the church and had never strayed too far from it. I'd never left the faith because of anger toward God or because I didn't see a reason for him in my life any longer. I didn't overcome some personal tragedy or misfortune involving a loved one. I wasn't freed from some horrendous sin. I hadn't overcome any dangerous addiction.

I felt I needed something like that in my story to have any kind of meaningful effect on the listener. I wanted a more compelling story that could really make a difference. One that could impact others in a profound way. I guess God heard my frustrations, because that's what he gave me.

I didn't know this before, but I now understand this truth about "testimonies." Whether we know it or not, we all have one. We all have a story to tell! Despite our selfish human natures and what the world is constantly telling us, our testimonies don't need an emotional plotline to affect people. In fact, our stories were never meant to be about us, and the simple story of finding Jesus and living a selfless life for him is powerful in and of itself and always worth telling.

There's No Such Thing as Perfect Faith

I'm not going to lie and say I showcased perfect faith throughout this whole traumatic experience, because I most certainly did not. In fact, I oftentimes found myself angry at God for what happened and was still happening. But I was still able to maintain some level of faith along this whole journey.

I often find myself thinking about the great men and women of faith we see in the Bible, their boldness, courage, fearlessness, and tenacity to pursue after what God had laid out for them. Mary, David, Joshua, Moses, Abraham, Peter, Paul, the list goes on. I often compare myself to these individuals. Maybe you've done the same. I tell myself I wish I was that bold and faithful. I wish I trusted God as unabashedly as they did. It's really easy for me to compare myself to those who have done things I yearn to do, not only in the Bible but also in day-to-day life.

But I have to constantly remind myself that these people were not perfect, and what I may perceive as a perfect and flawless life of faith and trust in God isn't actually that. They were human just like you and me. They made mistakes. They fell short. And they sometimes even chose wrongly.

By looking at these "heroes" of the Bible, I have learned that our faith doesn't always have to be a perfect faith to be real. In fact, it never will be, and the Bible shows that to be true (Eccles. 7:20).

All of these people did incredible things and had incredible faith, but they also had some incredibly deep imperfections. I say this not to expose their flaws so I can feel better about my own but to remind myself that we're all flawed and a little messy. There is no such thing as a flawless faith, and that should unite, not divide, Christians. We're all perfectly imperfect, journeying through this thing called faith together, one mistake and one victory at a time. If this wasn't the case, then we wouldn't have needed a perfect Savior, Jesus, to die on a cross and pay the penalty for all of our sins.

So no matter what you've got going on in life, whether your faith is as strong as it's ever been or as weak as it's ever felt, know that God is still God and his endless love for you stays the same. We all go through ups and down, highs and lows.

But don't ever give up because you're feeling down. God hasn't given up on you yet, so neither should you. Try to keep your head up high even through the lows. Try to keep your eyes open to God's goodness even when you feel like all you want to do is keep them closed. Keep your heart surrendered to him even when you feel like closing it off to the world.

> *Dear TBI,*
>
> *Do you remember the day we met? It was May 3, 2012. Actually, I don't recall meeting you that day, but that is when you first met Jacqui, Jayse, Jenna, and many of the rest of my friends and family. I didn't start getting to know you until a few weeks later. At first, I really didn't know who you were or understand you all that well. I certainly wasn't aware how much you would forever change my life. Don't get me wrong, I am most definitely grateful to be doing as well as I am because I know you have left others far worse off than me. But still, your presence has affected everything about me. You changed my life in ways I never could have imagined. You ultimately took away my ability to be a doctor, and I was forced to redefine myself. I had to find another purpose. I had to find what my doctors continually stressed to me, a "new normal." Because of you, there are some days I have a hard time recognizing the man I have become. So, in case you forgot, let me remind you again. You can leave at any time!*
>
> *—JEFF*

CHAPTER 3

This Isn't Normal

Jacqui Huxford

I t was a brisk, sunny morning in May. I woke up early for the second day of our neighborhood-wide garage sale. While I frantically moved about the house preparing for the sale, my husband helped our five-year-old son get ready and onto the bus for school. Our four-year-old daughter was glued to my side, interested in all the people browsing the sale, particularly the ones looking at the toys she had painstakingly chosen to part with.

While my daughter and I tended to the garage sale, my husband went to the local hardware store that my father happens to be part-owner of. My dad had mentioned that they had beautiful hanging baskets in stock, and we were in the market for some. Jeff left under strict instruction to send me pictures before purchasing the baskets since I couldn't go along. I guess I didn't really trust him to buy the baskets I wanted, but technology let me monitor his style decisions.

Fifteen minutes passed and Jeff called to discuss the hanging basket choices. I was happy he actually called instead of trying to figure it out on his own. Once we had decided, I hung up, knowing he would be home with them shortly. I never had any reason to be worried when Jeff would leave the house. He always came home and always showed up on time. Business picked up at our garage sale, and before I knew it an hour had gone by since I last spoke to my husband. This wasn't like Jeff, and I found myself a little worried. Normally, he would have called or texted me to let me know he was going to be late, but I hadn't heard anything from him.

A wave of nausea flooded the pit of my stomach. I didn't want to think something was wrong, but this was truly out of character for him. I wasn't going to allow my mind to run away with itself. I told myself he had just stopped in at his office on his way home and lost track of time as he chatted away. This would have been normal for him, but even then he would have texted me to at least let me know. I looked around to see that, for the first time all morning, I had not a single customer. Everyone had left, or at least they had bought everything worth buying. Jenna was out chasing butterflies in the yard with a neighbor boy, and I began processing whether or not I should start cleaning everything up and close down for the day. Then the phone rang. I expected it to be Jeff. I looked down at caller ID and felt my heart stop beating for what felt like an eternity. I quickly pushed aside any notion of danger as I answered the call from Jeff's office number.

Maybe his phone had died and he just wanted to check-in. Or maybe something else had happened . . .

I will never forget the sensation that plagued my body as my husband's business partner told me of Jeff's fate that day. As his words reached my ears, I found myself in a fog of utter disbelief and paralyzing fear. It was almost as if I was part of a movie. As his business partner was telling me what happened, life began to move in slow motion and I was trying to convince myself that what I was hearing wasn't true. "Jeff has been in a horrible car accident and has been airlifted to Advocate Christ Hospital," he said. I couldn't believe what I was hearing. Not my Jeff. There's no way. The tears came without warning. It was as if a dam broke on a lake I didn't know existed. This wasn't really happening. We were a young couple with two small children living the American dream. We had everything going for us. This couldn't really be happening to me. To us. To him. I had to force myself to focus on his words, "Wait, where was he taken again?" I asked. He repeated the name, but it didn't sound any more familiar. "Where is that?" I asked. "In Chicago," he said. Why Chicago? I wondered. I thanked him and somehow managed to end the conversation without completely losing it. God kept me focused and at peace. I still don't remember how I got everything done that day.

As I set the phone down, the world began spinning out of control. I thought of Jeff, the kids, our marriage, and all that God had done in our lives over the last few years. I had never been in a situation like this. What do I do now? Whom do I call? What do I do first? God, help me, I asked. I didn't know, but I did have enough wherewithal to call my neighbor who had been tending to her own garage sale that morning and ask her to come over immediately. I had no idea what I needed her to do; I just needed someone there to make sure I was making sane choices and to help if needed.

As she closed her garage and rushed over, my mind began to race, trying to land on logic and truth. What do I do now? I had just heard the most earth-shattering news. This isn't an ordinary accident. The walls were caving in around me, but I had a family to care for and a husband to tend to. I had to maintain focus. As soon as my neighbor reached my garage, she hugged me with deep sympathy. She had never been in a situation quite like this one and was unsure what to tell me to do, which is actually better than her trying to lie to me. Sometimes when things go wrong, you just need a hug and someone to tell you they love you. We decided my next step should be to close my garage door, thus closing the sale. As the door descended, my daughter came around the corner with an inquisitive look, wondering why we were closing the door on her. That's when she noticed my tear-stained face and red, puffy eyes. I reached for her, telling her that her daddy had been in a bad car accident and we needed to go to the hospital. She looked stunned and confused, and very unsure of what all of this meant. I was at a loss, not knowing how to explain the gravity of this situation to my innocent and naïve four-year-old.

I picked up the phone to call my mom; no answer. How could my mom not pick up the phone at a time like this? I tried again. "Hello, Mom. Jeff has been in a horrible car accident and has been airlifted to Advocate Christ Hospital. That's all I know," I said. "I'm already on my way, someone from the office called and let me know so I could make sure I was there for you," she said. "Ok, hurry!" I replied.

My next phone call was to Jeff's mom. No answer. Of all days for no one to pick up their phone. I called Jeff's dad. "Hello." With a voice shaken by tears, I said, "Hi, this is Jacqui. I have some bad news. Jeff has been in a horrible car accident and has been airlifted to a hospital in Chicago. That is all they told me." "I'm so sorry!" he replied. "I'm so sorry, Jacqui!" "It isn't your fault," I told him. "What should we do?" he asked. I said, "You need to pack a bag and get in the car and come up here." I gave him the name of the hospital and hung up the phone.

My mom arrived and held me in her arms for a few minutes while I tried to understand what was happening. She told me she had driven past the scene of the accident and that it didn't look good. I told her I didn't know what to do. I didn't know whether to bring the kids with me or find someone to watch them. Something inside me told me I needed to have my kids with me. What if the news was bad? What if they needed to say goodbye to their daddy today? I had to bring them because I couldn't live with the guilt of not having them with me if something went wrong. So we called Jayse's elementary school to have them get him ready to check out.

My mom called my dad and told him to meet us back at the house in fifteen minutes. Then she, Jenna, and I headed to the school to pick Jayse up. I went with the secretary to his classroom, explaining to several teachers and staff on the way the reason for my distraught and tear-stained face. His teacher hugged me and told me she would be praying, and we headed back home to figure out what to do next. I had forgotten to put my wedding ring on that morning, and as weird as it sounds, I was insistent that we needed to go back to the house to get it before heading to the hospital. I can't really explain the logic in that decision; it just felt like I needed to somehow be connected with Jeff. So we drove back for my ring. I know there is a deeper symbolism there, I just haven't yet discovered it, and maybe I never will.

My dad drove the five of us to the hospital. The direction we had to go meant we would have to drive through the busy intersection that had rocked our world that day. As we drove up to the scene, the red truck that had t-boned my husband was staring straight at us, almost in a "you think this truck is bad, wait until you see the other one" kind of way. My eyes could not believe the destruction they were seeing. It almost seemed fake and too crazy to be real. The entire front end of the red truck was smashed in. I didn't want to look at Jeff's truck, but I couldn't pull my eyes away . . . I had to see how bad it was. His black truck leaned halfway off the road, wrapped around a concrete pole on the driver side. The entire top half of his truck had been lifted off. The passenger side was completely caved in from the impact of the red truck. It didn't seem possible that there would be any survivors from the sea of metal destruction before me. Strangely enough, I felt an immense calm rooted in my bones that would not allow my mind to run away with itself. God kept me sane. There is no other explanation. I could take the news, whatever it may be, as it came and deal with it as needed. I would not proceed to guess what his injuries might include. I would remain rational and calm. It was the only way I could keep myself from spiraling out of control. I would trust that God had this all under control.

After multiple fruitless attempts to call and get more information about Jeff from the hospital, I decided to wait to hear the news once we arrived. I believe this was God protecting me from having my mind run wild if the doctors actually told me what was going on and how severe his injuries were. It was the longest hour and a half drive of my life. Every red light felt like an eternity. Every minute passing meant one less minute I could be with Jeff, one minute of time taken from my children to spend with their potentially dying father. And that truly broke my heart. I had to be strong for my kids, but I also didn't want to lie to them and act like everything was okay. Daddy was hurt, and I needed them to be praying for him just as much as I was. We were a family, and we needed to stick together.

We finally arrived at the hospital and went straight to the ER. One of our pastors was already there to offer support. The front desk informed me that Jeff was getting an MRI and someone would be with me momentarily to give more information on his condition. I felt like I had been waiting forever. A few minutes later a woman stepped out into the waiting room and called my name. I thought to myself, "OK, this is it. You are about to find out the fate of your husband. Be strong . . . by the grace of God, you can get through this."

I entered that room to hear the news . . . alone. I am not sure if everyone thought I wanted to go into that room alone or if it all just happened so fast that no one realized. I just told myself that was OK; I can handle this and steeled myself as the doctor told me the news. It was another one of those life-stands-still moments where you can't believe this is really happening to you. She said something to the effect of, "When you see Jeff you will notice he has a large hematoma (swelling) on the left side of his head due to the fact that his head hit a cement pole. He also has a couple of broken ribs, one of which punctured his lung and caused it to collapse, which is why he has a chest tube. You will also notice an interosseous on his upper arm. They had trouble finding his veins in the field and, therefore, put a line directly into a bone in his arm." She paused and looked at me. "Do you have any questions?" I sat there dumbfounded; my thoughts seemed so inappropriate as I sat there thinking, "Is that it?" I had seen the destruction both vehicles had endured. How was it possible that he didn't have more broken bones, visible wounds, or need some kind of surgery? I almost felt a sense of relief in that moment. "Can I see him?" I asked.

She led me back through a corridor of hallways. People were everywhere. The rooms were full. Several beds were pushed up against the walls of the hallway. A wave of nausea passed through my stomach as she turned and headed into one of the rooms. What would he look like? Would I even recognize him? What would I do? Did they prepare me enough for what I was about to see?

No. The answer is no. They did not prepare me enough. No one can ever be prepared to walk into a room and see your husband lying in a hospital bed hooked to a machine helping him breathe. He was partially sedated but still moving in such a way that made it appear he was in extreme pain and constant discomfort. His legs kept bending and turning, his arms and chest not finding rest. He moaned as he searched for relief. His hands were encompassed in what looked like large padded mittens connected to the bed to keep him from pulling out the various tubes attached to him. (He had already pulled out his chest tube before arriving.) I couldn't breathe. I felt the walls coming in around me. My whole world came crashing down. I took a deep breath. A sixth sense kicked in and I felt an overwhelming need to comfort him . . . as best I could. I sat by his bedside telling him over and over again that I was here and that everything would be okay.

I couldn't believe how quickly life had changed. In one day we went from the family who had it all to sitting in a hospital wondering if we were about to lose Jeff. After a few minutes, I returned to the waiting room to relay the news. Those who had come to see him took turns going back to be with him. My children, unsure of all that was happening around them, were stuck in the waiting room wanting to see their father so badly but hearing over and over again that it would be too scary for them to see their daddy that way. Jayse would say, "But, Mommy, I'm tough. I can handle it. I want to see Daddy!" Sometimes it is so hard to be the parent, having to deny your children something they want because you know it is in their best interest but feeling the pain of their heartbreak when you tell them no. Seeing Daddy would have to wait. I didn't want them to see him like this. And if something tragic were to happen, I didn't want them to remember him like this. Several people came and went that day. My brother and sister-in-law took my kids to their house for the night.

It was a long night. We watched Jeff writhe in pain for sixteen hours, unable to tell any of us where he was hurting. The hard chairs we sat in provided no comfort, and the tiredness from the day's events hung heavy on my eyes. Finally, the news came that they would be moving him to his own room in ICU.

The move sent us to another waiting room. This one proved to be much quieter. We rested as best we could that first night. The pain and anxiety each family in the waiting room was experiencing was overwhelming. There were two other individuals in the ICU who had a large number of visitors. The waiting room was packed, busy, and emotionally overpowering.

Jeff was finding it difficult to relax. He couldn't breathe well due to his collapsed lung, which continued to fill with fluid. His breathing was labored and originated from his stomach rather than his chest. He had no use of his hands and his legs were secured to the bed but somehow he still found a way to use his feet to pull out his catheter multiple times. His tongue was swollen and bloody because he had bitten it either during the accident or during a seizure shortly after. He would wake up every once in a while and open his eyes, but it was like he was staring right through us.

There was a two-hour period of time each day in the ICU that visitors were not allowed. This rule was put in place to give the patients time to rest. I used this time to try to nap. I felt a sense of relief each day when this time came because I could take a few minutes to breathe. During Jeff's stay at the hospital, I often had to leave the room to give my mind and heart a break. The agony of sitting by his bedside for hours on end each day really got to me, so it was important for me to take this time to gather myself emotionally. Fluid continued to build up in Jeff's lungs. They had to suction them every hour. He would get very agitated and sweaty when the nurse did this. He was also given breathing treatments in which a machine literally shook his entire upper body to try to prevent pneumonia. I can only imagine what those felt like to a body that had just experienced a horrific car accident, his brain in a complete fog, with multiple broken ribs he was trying to recover from. Needless to say, he hated the treatments, and it was hard to watch.

I did not go home for the first time until three days after the accident. It was extremely tough to leave. I felt so torn between two places. I wanted to be there for my husband, but I also wanted to go home to be with my children. They still were not allowed to see their dad, so it had been three days without Mom or Dad for them. I cried as we pulled away from the hospital, second guessing my decision to leave. The one and a half hour drive one-way is brutal and feels like a complete waste of precious time.

Walking into our home was excruciatingly hard. To be in our house filled with reminders of Jeff and not having him physically there was gut-wrenching. I put our children to bed, way past their bedtime, and made my way downstairs. As I sat on the cold tile floor in the kitchen, I sorted through his personal items they had sent home with me: cut-off underwear and shorts, his wedding ring, his socks and shoes, nail clippers, lip balm, and a pocket knife. I sobbed as I allowed the gravity of what had happened hit me like a ton of bricks. I had never felt so alone in all my life. Yet I knew that God heard my cries. I knew he would never leave me or forsake me. I knew he was working. Those comforts are what finally allowed me to sleep. I know God is working even when we perceive that he is silent. He is with us, comforting us, working in our lives, and working all things together for the good of those who are in Christ Jesus.

Progress

The first time Jeff got out of his bed was four days after his accident. He was placed in an upright position in a chair next to his bed. His nurse said that to him this felt like running a marathon. He hadn't had any nutrition since the accident and didn't have a feeding tube put in until the fourth day.

Jeff couldn't think clearly and the responses to the few questions he could answer were vague. For example, someone would point to me and ask Jeff, "Who is this?" He would pause and then reply "Wife." That was all he could remember. He knew I was his wife, but he could not remember my name.

Jeff spent four days in the ICU. While we were there I learned that he had suffered a Diffuse Axonal Injury (DAI) to his brain, also known as brain shearing.

Diffuse axonal injury isn't the result of a blow to the head. Instead, it results from the brain moving back and forth in the skull as a result of acceleration or deceleration.

- *Automobile accidents*

- *Sports-related accidents*

- *Violence*

- *Falls*

- *Child abuse such as Shaken Baby Syndrome*

When acceleration or deceleration causes the brain to move within the skull, axons, the parts of the nerve cells that allow neurons to send messages between them, are disrupted. As tissue slides over tissue, a shearing injury occurs. This causes the lesions that are responsible for unconsciousness, as well as the vegetative state that occurs after a severe head injury.

A diffuse axonal injury also causes brain cells to die, which cause swelling in the brain. This increased pressure in the brain can cause decreased blood flow to the brain, as well as additional injury. The shearing can also release chemicals which can contribute to additional brain injury.[3]

Jeff had lost communication to portions of his brain, and it would be quite a while before we would know how bad the injury was. The doctor told me, "What you are going to need is a lot of patience during his recovery because it will be a long, slow process." "That's good," I said, "because patience is typically something I have a lot of." I had no idea just how much patience his recovery would require!

He spent three days in a step-down unit (from the ICU). He still was not talking much, maybe a word here or there. During this time period he was often found moving, fidgeting, moaning in pain. When he was first transferred to the step-down unit, they gave him a drug called Haldol that basically turned him into a zombie. It was awful what that medicine did to him. He was completely in another world, would drool constantly out of the side of his mouth, and his arms and legs remained strapped to the bed.

And to make matters worse, the visitors of a stabbing victim in the next room over stole my wallet from my purse. I was forced to cancel all credit and bank cards, leaving me with virtually no access to money. This was one of the lowest

---

3   "Diffuse Axonal Injury," *BrainandSpinalCord.org*. Accessed November 14, 2017. http://www.brainandspinalcord.org/diffuse-axonal-injury/.

times of this whole ordeal. How could someone prey on someone else during a time like this? Why would God allow this to happen to me now? Still, I rested in the assurance that he knew what I was enduring. He understood my pain and would bring us through this.

Jayse and Jenna didn't get to see their dad until he was transferred to the step-down unit. This was because I didn't want them to be scared. I told them that Daddy would look different because he had a big bump on his head and doctors have his hands in big, puffy gloves. I also told them that he isn't the same Daddy we know right now because he hit his head and he doesn't feel great, but he really wanted to see them. Jayse put on his little five-year-old brave face and walked right into the room with me. I could sense his trepidation, but he really wanted to do what was best for his dad. Jenna wouldn't step foot into the room. She took one look at her dad and got scared. She knew that wasn't truly him. It was so hard to watch one child wrestle with her fear and choose to run and another wrestle with discomfort and choose to be strong.

Jeff was unable to eat for the majority of his stay at the first hospital. His body was dwindling down to nothing. He was hours away from getting a feeding tube put directly into his stomach because he kept pulling out the feeding tube placed through his nose down to the stomach, but then he finally began to eat some soft foods. He began occupational, speech, and physical therapy, which consisted of attempting to take a few steps down the hallway while being held at the waist with a harness to prevent falls. He tired so quickly from the pain and lack of energy from not eating that this therapy never lasted long. Advocate Christ Hospital decided he would need to be transferred to a more long-term care hospital for brain injuries. We moved onto the tenth floor of the Shirley Ryan AbilityLab (formerly Rehabilitation Institute of Chicago) one week after the accident.

They gave us a tour of his floor to show us where everything was located. Their facility would help him relearn how to walk on his own, push him to work on his speaking, and help him figure out how to function in his day-to-day reality. After meeting the doctors, therapists, and some of the staff, I was confident this facility was exactly what Jeff needed.

Exhaustion was setting in for me. It was all such a whirlwind! I would go home each night and find his clothes and shoes sitting there. I would have flashbacks to moments and memories when he was home, normal, himself. I longed for those days and, at times, had to remind myself that I don't get to wake up from this nightmare. This is our new reality. I must trust in the Lord with all my heart and lean not on my own understanding.

For many days there was minimal response from Jeff. He would stare right through me most of the time. Every once in a while he would notice me, realize who I was, and pull me close, but as quick as it came, it was gone. He would not sit still; he would constantly try to get up out of his bed. One day, while changing his diaper, I felt such sorrow in that moment. I knew it would mortify him to know what was happening if he were in his right mind. I couldn't help but ask myself, "Is this what the rest of our lives are going to be like?"

Jeff was restless and agitated. He would repeatedly stand up, walk to the couch, sit down, stand up, walk to the bed, sit down, take pants off, put pants on, take pants off, put pants on . . . over and over and over again. He wasn't supposed to walk around without help, so we couldn't leave him alone. When he was in his wheelchair, he would move himself around using his feet to walk himself to the next hard surface. He would place his head in his hands and rest on top of the surface for a few seconds, then he would move on to find the next surface and repeat the same behavior.

Since Jeff couldn't be left alone, they put a large tent over the top of his bed that only zipped from the outside. Even though I understood the need for it, it felt so inhumane to zip him up in his bed each night.

It was a week and a half until I could be with my husband for an entire day without visitors. That first day with just us together was much needed! It was so quiet and peaceful, and Jeff was so calm.

Jenna still had not gone in to see her dad. He had developed a case of MRSA (an infection caused by a staph bacteria) and it had been quite a few days since the kids had been allowed at the hospital. Jenna told me one morning that she had a dream that Daddy came home but he talked funny. Poor kids . . . so much to deal with and try to understand.

There was a night I broke down thinking about how I wasn't able to lean on Jeff for support through this time. He was everything to me: my husband, my best friend, the father of my children, my confidant, my partner in crime, my bread winner, my support. And now I was left with none of that. I worried about how we were going to afford to keep our house and pay our bills. I thought about the people I had watched earlier on the city street holding hands and how I wasn't sure if Jeff and I would ever be able to do that again. I would find myself slipping into an alternate reality where this was no longer happening to me just to make it through a day. God remained faithful to me. He continued to provide.

People were very gracious and kind to us during this time. So many people brought us food, gift baskets, flowers, things for the kids to do, prayer shawls, and more. We had people buy hotel rooms for us, drive me to the hospital, wash our sheets, and watch our kids. We were beyond blessed. God provided for us through the many kind gestures of those who listened when he prompted them to respond to a friend in need.

Approximately thirteen days after the accident Jeff had a very encouraging day. Although the road ahead seemed to stretch endlessly, Jeff was able to hold his attention a little longer. He answered several questions and even asked a few of his own. They didn't make complete sense in the conversation, but we felt it was a step in the right direction. I longed to have a conversation with my husband that he would understand and recall within an hour of having the discussion. He cooperated during his therapies and was even able to walk down the hallway unassisted as long as we walked right beside him.

His sleep patterns were all out of whack. He would often leave his room at night and bother the nurses and then nap a lot during the day. His days and nights were mixed up. He had such a childlike nature about him. When I told him (because we had to retell him every day) that he was in a car accident, he looked at me like I was crazy and said, "I don't remember that!" When I told him he would get a new truck, he said, "Sweet!" We still didn't feel like "our Jeff" was there, but he was making progress in the right direction.

Jeff went through a period where he became very emotional. He would call people to talk with them for about a minute or two and would end up crying and telling them how thankful he was. Through the darkest of times, we were learning to find joy. We were thankful for the life God had spared. We were joyful for the provisions God was giving freely. Through the pain, joy emerged.

My brother and brother-in-law started a group called TJIJA. It stood for "Till Jeff Is Jeff Again." A group of men from our church and hometown, along with some of Jeff's friends, chose not to shave until Jeff came home from the hospital. Each time they would itch or really want to shave, they would pray for Jeff's recovery. When Jeff heard about this group, he wept. God was using our circumstances to grow not only our faith in him but to grow others' faith as well.

It wasn't until May 21, eighteen days after the accident, that Jenna would step foot in Jeff's room. She was very nervous, but as soon as she came into the room, Jeff sat up in his bed and said, "Jenna!" in his normal voice and tone she was used to. She warmed up to him immediately. She climbed onto his bed and hugged him.

The following week Jeff got to do some of his physical therapy outside. The rehab center is located right downtown in the Gold Coast, so going outside proved to be extremely tiring for Jeff, as he found himself quickly over-stimulated.

I stayed with Jeff in his room that night. I needed to run out to my car to get my overnight bag, so I had to zip Jeff up in his bed until I made it back up to his tenth-floor room. I told him I would be right back; I just had to run out to the car. When I came back, he had a panic-stricken look on his face and he was frantically trying to find a way to get out of the netted bed. Relief flooded his face as I entered and unzipped the bed. He said he needed to go to the bathroom and didn't want to wet himself. The following day we received news that he was no longer a fall risk and we got clearance to remove the enclosure over his bed. What great news!

Jeff continued doing work with the therapists. He did everything from learning to shop, wash himself, walk, exercise, categorize things, answer questions and then asked to recall information. He was finally cleared from his soft diet, and we received permission to go out to a restaurant for dinner. This proved to be difficult for Jeff, as the restaurant was loud and the over-stimulation exhausted him.

His doctor gave me the option of bringing Jeff home to continue his recovery process there, which many before me had tried and ended up wearing themselves out, or having Jeff go to a long-term facility indefinitely. They recommended the latter. They talked to me about my options; the closest facility was three hours (one way) from our home. I was so depressed to hear this news. I had no idea how I would manage to raise two children on my own, all the while trying to make trips to visit my husband three hours away to help with his recovery. I felt so helpless. This was going to be next to impossible and I wasn't sure how I would do it.

The next day the doctor came in to ask what my decision was, and I told him I had decided to take Jeff home. He began trying to talk me out of doing that, and then Jeff walked into the room. The doctor began talking to him and saw how Jeff had seemingly changed overnight. He was much more stable and his mind was working a little more clearly. It was as if Jesus had flipped a switch that gave Jeff enough boost in his recovery that we no longer even needed a long-term facility. God is so GOOD; he is so good to us!

I still noticed a very innocent, honest, childlike quality to Jeff. I wasn't sure how long his recovery would take, but I was thankful for what the Lord had done for us thus far and looked forward to how God could use us, and this situation, to further his kingdom here on earth. His progress was in baby steps, but it was moving in the right direction. God had blessed us with Jeff's life and we were eternally grateful.

On June 2, Jeff was released from the hospital. I was excited and terrified. This three-hour round trip had become my new normal for the past thirty days. Up to this point, the doctors and nurses had been taking care of him; now the burden would shift to my shoulders. Was I ready?

All I wanted to do, now that we were home, was take a break from the accident and its repercussions. I was tired;

tired of thinking about it, tired of talking about it, tired of explaining Jeff's progress to everyone. I was ready to move on. To live life. To have some normalcy. Jeff wanted to do nothing but talk about it. He wanted to hear about his hospital stay, about his medical issues, who visited him in the hospital, and how they reacted and what they said. He wanted to know and hear it all. He couldn't remember any of it. I remembered it all too well, and the last thing I wanted to do was relive it. I remained patient, knowing he needed time and probably needed to hear it all to help with the healing process.

We both needed time to figure out what our new life looked like now. Would he ever work again? Would he ever not need a nap in the afternoon? Would he ever have the energy to go out and work in the yard? Would he be able to handle the heat of the day so we could do things outside or go camping? Would he be able to handle large family gatherings where noise levels are high and energy abounds? Would he ever be able to drive or mow the lawn again? Question after unanswered question remained.

Though the path might be tough and the uncertainty excruciating at times, I trusted that the Lord was in control and would use this for his greater good. I rested in the hope we can claim in Jesus. He would show us a way where there was no way.

It was frustrating to have both Jeff and the kids home while we were not able to do any of the normal things we would have done together. He couldn't camp because it was too hot, too much work, and too much change. We couldn't go to the beach because of the heat. We couldn't go on vacation or go shopping because we needed to save our money. Jeff had not been working for two months now. All of our routines had changed. So little had returned to normal. The kids had missed half their baseball season. If I wanted to go anywhere by myself, I had to find someone to keep an eye on Jeff and the kids. Otherwise, we all had to go. Jeff couldn't drive or operate heavy machinery. He wasn't sleeping well, meaning I wasn't sleeping well either. The kids were disappointed every night that Daddy couldn't carry them upstairs for bed like he used to or go outside and play catch. We could not stay long at family gatherings or parties because it caused Jeff to tire quickly and feel overwhelmed. Life all around had changed for us, and it just plain stunk!

We felt God calling us to learn to be patient. We did *a lot* of waiting throughout his recovery. It was sixteen hours in the ER, a week and a half before we saw any part of the Jeff we knew, two weeks before he could remember why he was even in the hospital, three weeks before he could eat normal food, thirty days before he returned home from the hospital, five months before he could drive again, and six months before he could attempt to work. If we only knew how much more God had to teach us about being patient in the waiting!

CHAPTER 4

Getting Back to Normal

I had been in the hospital for roughly three weeks when I finally came out of my prolonged period of post traumatic amnesia (PTA), the period of time following a TBI during which you are not aware of who you are, where you're at, and why you're there. During this time, I started to realize that something significant had happened to me. I just wasn't yet aware of its magnitude. That came at a much later date.

As the fog of PTA lifted, I slowly began to understand what people were telling me when I would ask them what in the world had happened and what was going on. And, man, I sure had a lot of questions! After asking and talking to many family, friends, doctors, and workers at the hospital, I figured out that I had been in a car accident near my home and had suffered a traumatic brain injury. It took me a while to figure out where exactly the accident had occurred. I knew I had been nearly killed and was then lifelined by helicopter to a trauma hospital just outside of Chicago. I stayed at this first hospital for one week. Even to this day I have no recollection of ever being there. I was then transferred to the Rehab Institute of Chicago (now known as Shirley Ryan AbilityLab), where I received more intensive therapy.

The Good and the Bad of a Quick Recovery

I should mention here that a lack of self-awareness is a common effect of brain injuries. Many people who suffer a brain injury don't know anything has ever happened to them. They go on with their lives as if nothing has changed, potentially hurting themselves and others along the way. I felt very fortunate because, once I started my recovery, I believed my self-awareness was well intact. I was confident that this wasn't going to be a problem for me. I felt I had developed a good understanding of what happened and that it was something pretty serious. But I still really had no doubts that I could come back from it and make a full recovery.

*****

I remember my doctors telling me early on and repeatedly in my recovery that, following a brain injury, a person has to find a "new normal." My brain was so damaged that I would no longer be able to do the things I used to do. And I may not even want to. I may have a different personality. I could have new interests. In essence, most everything that defined me would change, and I would need to redefine who I was and who I wanted to be. But I wasn't buying any of this. I didn't want to believe them. I liked who I was before and I wasn't ready to give that up. I knew I could get it back. It would be like everything else in life to this point; I would just have to work hard for it. That's what I believed so that's what I did. I set out to prove them wrong and get back the "normal" they said I couldn't have.

And once my recovery started, it seemed to go very fast. I was able to go home with my family after just one month of outpatient therapy and didn't have to go to a long-term rehab facility. When I returned home, things continued to go very well. You see, it had been assumed that I would likely never practice medicine again because of the severity of my brain injury. But because of my quick and miraculous recovery, I was not only able to return to work, I was able to return much faster than anyone expected. I was back to work as a doctor in just five months. With my quick return to working at a job that depended solely on my brain power—the thing my doctors had told me would be forever lessened—I was now extra confident they had been wrong about their whole idea of a "new normal." They underestimated who I was. I was the exception. I would be the anomaly.

I am thankful for my quick recovery, but it ultimately gave me false hope for my future. It perpetuated my overconfidence that I could defy the odds and return to "normal." I believed my recovery would continue at its fast pace, and I would be back to who I was before in no time. But this wasn't the case, and when this didn't happen, I felt like a failure. I thought I wasn't working hard enough. I would later figure out the truth: no matter how hard or how long I worked to get back to "normal," it just wasn't attainable. Maybe I wasn't nearly as aware of my "new" self as I thought I was.

But my overconfidence was perpetuated even more when I returned to see my rehab doctor, Dr. Brkic, two months after my accident for a regular check-up. He was very pleased with my recovery and even moved up my repeat neuropsych test to evaluate my capacity to work. He told me that he had taken care of two other doctors with a brain injury, neither as severe as mine, and they were never able to return to work, so I shouldn't get my hopes up. But he had a feeling that I might just do it.

I returned for my neuropsych test to see if and when I could go back to work. Surprisingly, I passed and was cleared to go back on a "work trial" with reduced hours, reduced patient load, and close supervision. Even under these conditions, I was working, and that wasn't supposed to happen. I quickly expanded my hours and required less supervision, although I didn't attain the same patient numbers as before. But all of this good news led me to believe that I would soon be back to full capacity at work.

I even remember what a resident physician said to me one day. He had looked at my files before seeing me, and when he walked into the room he couldn't believe I was the guy he had just read about. All his positive feedback reinforced my false overconfidence. I was going to get back "normal." There was still nothing telling me it couldn't be done. At least not yet. I had already tested out of occupational therapy (OT), and I only needed one more month of outpatient physical therapy (PT). Speech therapy (ST) was a different story.

I had been functioning well in the home setting, so I initially did ST for only a couple months. I figured this meant I was doing really well and had no major problems. But when I went back to work, I realized I needed some more work. I was having a difficult time finding the right words to explain things to patients and answering their questions. I was having problems with my critical thinking. Looking back, I think this may have been the first sign that the normal I was after was going to be tougher to get back than I thought, maybe even impossible.

Depression, Anxiety, OCD, and ADD: Becoming the Patient

When I left the hospital after my accident, my number one priority was to get back to the old Jeff—the one with the healthy brain, ability to multitask, quick wit, great sense of humor (*that one is still up for debate!*), calm disposition, and easygoing personality. I wanted that guy back, and I was going to do everything I could to find him. But after about a year of relentless attempts, I figured out this just wasn't going to happen. When the weight of this reality hit me, I became depressed. This was something I had never personally experienced before. And because I wasn't used to feeling depressed, this also caused significant anxiety and worry. It was one of the most difficult times of my life. I believe the primary cause of this—in addition to my damaged brain structure—was that I had set unattainable goals for myself. And when I couldn't reach them, I felt like a failure. I was hard on myself, becoming my own worst enemy and constantly berating myself for not being the man I yearned to be. This went on for quite some time before I sought help. The whole experience made me realize how hard mental health problems are to handle. I began to feel truly sad and compassionate for the millions of people around the world who struggle daily with some type of mental illness.

Life was difficult during this period. I wasn't motivated. I didn't think highly of myself. Depression and anxiety do that to you; they lie to you in hopes that you'll believe them. And I did, for a while; it wasn't until I started to share my hurts and struggles with others that I started to get better. It took a change in my mindset, which was aided by medications and counseling. I eventually began reconfiguring my unhealthy way of thinking and living.

I think this started when I finally admitted that TBI had forever changed me and I was going to be different. I owned it and accepted it. I had new interests. I had a new personality. And no matter how much effort I put into it, I wasn't going back to who I was before. I am not implying that TBI survivors should stop working to get better, but they need to be wise and focus on who they are now and improving that which can be improved. TBI survivors don't need to spend any time trying to reach their old selves. It's never going to work, and it's not who they are anymore.

*****

I remember going back to the Rehab Institute of Chicago to follow up with my doctors and being asked on several different occasions if I was having any symptoms of depression or anxiety. I now understand why they were being so persistent. Statistics show that one year after a brain injury, more than 50 percent of survivors are affected by anxiety and depression, and after seven years that number jumps to more than 66 percent. The general population rate is less than 10 percent.

I was naive and believed these statistics wouldn't apply to me. I had never dealt with any mental health issues. And why would I start now? I had so many things to be happy about and thankful for. I had just survived a near-fatal car accident and my recovery was going better than any of my doctors expected. I had great friends and a wonderful family. I was back to working as a family doctor, a job I knew and loved. And most importantly, I was a Christian, and Christians aren't supposed to deal with that stuff!

But none of these things seemed to matter! I was still having a hard time accepting my new life and the new me. I wasn't sure how to act or how I was supposed to function as the person I had suddenly become. I wasn't even sure I liked who I had turned into.

I started dealing with emotions and feelings that I never had before. I was becoming depressed because of all the effort it took to function as normal as possible. I was depressed because I wasn't the same husband, father, doctor, family member, or friend that I used to be, and I never would be again.

I also started having anxiety. Most of it was social anxiety and worrying about what others were thinking of me. Were they watching me and judging me? Did they think I was faking my injuries, because I certainly had no scars to show them? Sometimes I felt anxious for no reason at all.

All this confusion and questioning, combined with the structural damage and changes to my brain from the accident, led to depression and anxiety. After denying they existed for some time, I finally admitted to having them and knew I needed to seek help. Now, I had been treating these conditions for years as a family doctor, but after experiencing it myself, I became shamefully aware of how poorly I understood it. Although no two people experience mental illness in the same way, I was getting a glimpse of how some of my patients felt. In addition to this, I always struggled to understand and explain to them why the medications I was prescribing or the counseling I was suggesting for their conditions could help.

My treatment for the past five years has included both medication and psychotherapy (cognitive behavioral therapy, or CBT), and if I was still practicing medicine, I would happily tell my patients what the treatments have done for me and what they could potentially do for them. The combination of the two have helped me accept the things I really had no control over and motivated me to work on the things I do. My psychologist uses CBT to help me deal with the drastic life changes and to help me combat the resultant unhealthy thinking patterns. In addition to these, regular exercise, the proper amount of sleep, and a healthy diet have also been important in improving my mental health. Depression and anxiety are something I will continue to battle, but I am extremely grateful to have found ways to do so.

Besides the depression and anxiety, which were both brand new for me, I started having problems with obsessive-compulsive disorder (OCD). Looking back, I think this actually started when I was still in the hospital. I remember coming home from the hospital looking through a box containing all the cards people sent to me while I there. I came across a scrap piece of paper on which I had written down the names of several people—adults and children—some I knew well and some I hardly knew. I asked my wife if she knew what it was. She said it was something I did at night when I was trying to remember names of people and how they were related to each other. It was something I was quite "obsessed" with remembering and there was really no reason for it. I think this was the very beginning of my new battle with OCD.

The OCD that came as a result of my TBI was not a welcome addition to my life, but I think it was, in some ways, instrumental in my return to medicine. As a family practice doctor, you are required to remember a lot of details about a lot of things. You have to stay organized and successfully multitask. OCD gave me to ability to do both of these. But because it was so very wearing on me, and probably my coworkers as well, it was not sustainable to continue as a doctor.

OCD wasn't something that just affected me at work. I carried it home with me. This displayed itself in many ways. When I saw someone out in public and couldn't remember their name, I would dwell on figuring out what it was until I did so. If I made a to-do list for the day, I would not be satisfied until I had completed everything on that list. (*Side note: Does anybody else do something and after they have done it, add it to your to-do list so you can mark it off?*)

OCD has affected my flexibility, and I don't mean my ability to stretch or do the splits. I am talking about my ability to "go with the flow." I need structure and organization. The opposite of that causes me a lot of stress, which affects my ability to function. I have thus become rather rigid in my daily behaviors and rituals..

I also hate losing things or misplacing something. I can think of one instance when I lost the remote control (and I don't even watch much television). Jacqui left the house while I was looking for it. When she returned home a couple hours later, I was still trying to find it. I knew it wasn't a big deal, but I couldn't let it go. We had always kind of joked about me being OCD, but when this happened we both decided it was something I should take more seriously and talk to my doctors about.

I was seeing a psychologist at the time and talked to her about my concerns, and she agreed with my self-diagnosis. She taught me strategies using CBT to help deal with my OCD. One of the important things she taught me is to keep things in perspective. Is something really that important? And do I really have any control over it? She also showed me how I often think in extremes and how I need to instead think of the most likely conclusion. Using these strategies, when

I do, helps me. I know I am using the past tense like I have this thing all figured out, but OCD is something I still battle.

Eventually, I also began having problems with attention deficit disorder (ADD). I was having a very difficult time focusing on a task or concentrating for any period of time. I was very inattentive to what my wife and children were saying to me. I was very "scatterbrained." This was becoming very bothersome to me, my family, and my friends. When I explained these symptoms to my doctor, I began to get treated for ADD as well.

All of these health concerns were just more evidence that the normal I once knew wasn't my normal now.

God Uses Flawed People

Mental illness is now a part of my story, and it is something I have chosen to openly accept and courageously fight. A vital part of my acceptance has come from studying the Bible and understanding it in ways I never had before. In reading the Bible, I repeatedly came across people who dealt with mental illness. Growing up in church, I wasn't aware of this. The churches I went to just didn't talk about it that much, or maybe I wasn't paying close enough attention! So because of my ignorance, I was under the impression the people I heard about in the Bible were free of any sort of problems. And if I was living the way God wanted, I shouldn't have any problems either. I have learned this is simply not true! The Bible is full of people suffering from all sorts of issues. But many of them chose to stop carrying the burden themselves and to let God carry them through whatever they were struggling with. And that is what I am learning to do.

Illness of all kinds, both physical and mental, was not part of God's original plan. It exists because of sin. Thankfully, we have a God who loved us so much he came to rescue us from this mess. God sent Jesus, who lived a spotless life and died for our sins so that one day we can live forever in a perfect world free of all disease. This is one of God's promises, and it's in this promise that I place my hope and trust. But until that glorious day, there will be trials. There will be sickness. It is during these difficult times I find my hope, strength, and courage in another one of God's promises. The promise that in my weakness, he will carry me. I've never truly had to experience this until my accident. It wasn't an easy pill to swallow, and I believe weakness never really is. Why? Because our innate human nature tells us to keep from admitting our weaknesses and failures. Pride doesn't want us to admit these faults, but it doesn't mean they aren't there. The reality is, God specializes in using people who are broken, messed up, and flawed.

In the Bible, we see this happen through people like Moses, a man who wasn't the world's greatest leader, nor was he a very good speaker, but God used him in his weakness, equipped him with the strength and glory of God, and helped him lead God's people to the Promised Land. Moses did this in God's strength, not his own.

If you ever feel like you aren't worthy enough, remember that Jesus used a bunch of flawed people to share hope to a flawed world. In him we find renewal and mending. Jesus didn't call the equipped; he equips the called. And no matter what you've been through in life, remember that the same power that conquered the grave lives within you.

Each time he said, "My grace is all you need. My power works best in weakness." So now I am glad to boast about my weaknesses, so that the power of Christ can work through me. That's why I take pleasure in my weaknesses, and in the insults, hardships, persecutions, and troubles that I suffer for Christ. For when I am weak, then I am strong. (2 Cor. 12:9–10, NLV)

Some More Random Observations on My "New Normal"

- I can be pretty tiring to be around. I'm a bit of a prima donna, but I am, overall, less social than I used to be and prefer to be alone.
- I am much more serious.
- I don't joke around as much as I used to.
- I can't handle small talk.
- I need to have fewer options because I have difficulty making decisions (e.g., wearing the same type of outfits every day).
- I tend to take things personally even when they aren't meant to be hurtful or even directed at me.
- I can't have conversations in loud places.
- I am startled by sudden, loud noises.

- I can't multitask.
- Due to my poor short-term memory, I fear forgetting something, which leads me to dwell on whatever that is while neglecting everything else going on around me.
- I repeat questions to people to make sure I heard them correctly and to make sure I remember what was said.
- From a physical standpoint, I can't exercise like I used to (not that I was ever a fitness buff). I can walk and do things like yoga, but anything much more than that causes migraine headaches or extreme dizziness. My balance issues affect my ability to play sports with the kids.
- I have to sit on aisle seats because of claustrophobia, which changes the way my family and I deal with going places.
- We had bought a pop-up camper prior to my accident and were planning on using that regularly. After my accident, the thought of packing up, setting up, taking down, traveling with, and sleeping in a camper stressed me out, so I sold it.
- I also got stressed when the lawn needed mowing, and this would be on my mind when I was at work, so I decided to sell the mower and hire a mowing service.

Learning from Others Who Found Their "New Normal"

Katherine Wolf, a courageous stroke survivor, says this in her book *Hope Heals*[4] about her experience:

> *I can give God the glory, and it can still hurt. I used to cry myself to sleep every night. But I have learned, above all other lessons, that healing for each of us is spiritual. We will be fully restored in heaven, but we are actually healed on earth right now. My experience has caused me to redefine healing and to discover a hope that heals the most broken places: our souls.*

Tragedy does that to us. Sometimes it will force us to engage in life differently than we did before. This isn't a bad thing. It's just the way life works, and there is nothing we can do about it. We have to realize that there is a new way of life waiting for us, and if we rely on God and trust in his promises, this way of life can be just as fulfilling, if not more so, than our previous life. I believe this to be true, and it's because I am now living that new life.

Bethany Hamilton, in her book *Soul Surfer*[5], said:

---

4   Katherine Wolf and Jay Wolf, *Hope Heals: A True Story of Overwhelming Loss and Overcoming Love* (Zondervan, 2016).

5   Bethany Hamilton and Rich Bundschuh, *Soul Surfer: A True Story of Faith, Family, and Fighting to Get Back on the Board* (MTV Books, 2006).

Surfing isn't the most important thing in life. Love is. I've had the chance to embrace more people with one arm than I ever could with two.

Bethany's story is tragic to say the least, but it is also so powerful that it became a best-selling book and major motion picture. She lost her arm to a shark attack in a wild surfing accident, but she didn't let her tragedy keep her from finding joy, peace, and fulfillment in life. Did she have struggles along the way? Of course. Did she perhaps doubt her purpose in life? I assume so. But she kept moving forward, embraced what had taken place, and began searching for her "new normal." Her life may never be the same as it was when she had both arms, but that doesn't mean her life is no longer fulfilling and incredible. She chased after the new life awaiting her, gave God the glory for what she has overcome, and continues to inspire people around the world.

She is still surfing to this day, but she doesn't surf the way she used to. She had to learn how to surf differently because of her accident, and her new normal was a learning process. It didn't happen overnight. It came with great difficulty, struggle, and pain. But she never gave up. She had people around her who supported her in every way, helped her through the tough times, and cheered her on in the good times. She fully engaged her new normal, and because of this, went on to become one of the world's greatest surfers, even after losing one of her arms.

Besides the stories of other courageous people who have overcome great difficulties, I've always found encouragement and strength in the scriptures. Psalm 46:1–3 (NIV) is a wonderful reminder that God is always by our side.

God is our refuge and strength, an ever-present help in trouble. Therefore we will not fear, though the earth give way and the mountains fall into the heart of the sea, though its waters roar and foam and the mountains quake with their surging.

CHAPTER 5

Admitting, Defining, and Accepting Normal

I finally admitted I had a "new normal," but I still wasn't sure what that meant for me. I started to realize that normal is such a subjective term. Despite this realization, however, I was still spending a lot of time and energy trying to "define" what my "new normal" was supposed to look like. Where was I headed? What would my daily routines be? Where would I work? How would I provide for my family? I wanted to know what the future held and how to get there. I knew it was going to be different, but I didn't want to wait to find out the details. I wanted to know now. But it didn't happen. Instead, I was given time to rest and slow down, something I wasn't really used to. Since graduating from high school, I had been working toward the next degree, the next job, the next season of life. This accident forced me to slow down. And as hard as it was, I know it was good for my soul. I know it had a purpose.

All throughout the New Testament we see Jesus take time out of his busy life to rest, to pray, and rejuvenate his soul (Mark 6:31, Mark 1:35, Luke 5:16), and I believe this paints a beautiful picture for how we, as his followers, should take care of our own lives. Why? Because even the Son of God needed rest, so why would we think we're any different? We're not. We must learn to rest, to press pause, and to give ourselves opportunities to be refueled by the love and grace of Jesus. You can only go for so long until you need to be refilled.

Time to Accept

Admitting. Defining. And now even resting. Accepting was the next thing I needed to do. I needed to engage in the new life God had for me and make the best of it. Thrive in it. I had to act upon it, not just verbally agree to it. I needed to strive after the hope of God, the hope that is an anchor for our souls (Heb. 6:19), and trust that he would take care of me through it all.

So I started the process of accepting the new me. Something I should have started doing a long time ago. I began to focus less on my weaknesses, more on what strengths I still had and even ones I had gained. I was relearning who I was in life. I was relearning what it meant to be a husband, a dad, and a man of God. I became okay with being different. Once I did this, I started looking for ways to utilize my new strengths. I realized that even though I was changed, I still had a purpose, that God could still use me in mighty ways.

I Didn't Feel "Lucky"

Survivors of traumatic brain injuries recognize that they are fortunate to have survived their brain injury because, typically, whatever caused it could have easily taken their life. Most people feel the same way and will often remind them how "lucky" they are, but they will begin to feel guilty because they don't feel very lucky. They are also confused because, even though they may look the same, inside they're not sure who they are.

Despite all my positivity and upbeat talk of admitting and accepting my new "normal," I certainly didn't feel very lucky, as so many other well-meaning people were innocently suggesting to me. But, eventually, I started to move past my self-pity and find my purpose once again. But my purpose was only found after I let go of who I used to be and accepted who I am now. This is when God came in and completely turned my life around.

An Awakening That Would Lead to My Acceptance of My "New Normal"

I am sure most of you are familiar with Saul's story of change when he met Jesus on the road to Damascus. I don't have quite that dramatic of a story, but I do have one. I can't say I saw any vision or heard a voice, but something amazing did happen, and it changed me. Paul was someone who once killed Christians before his transformation with Jesus, and although he and I don't have the same past experiences, we've both found transformation through God.

I had just taken my Family Medicine Certification Examination, which I passed, but it was significantly tougher for me than the first time I had taken it. My recall and memory were just not the same. I think I had enough still in my long-term memory, and that's what carried me through. After the exam, Jacqui and I flew to Dallas, Texas, to attend a conference for her work. At the time, Jacqui was working at our church as the director of Small Group Life, and the conference we were attending was organized by RightNow Media, an online streaming library of content for local churches.

I was going to there with no expectations other than it being a nice little getaway. Maybe I would hear a few good speakers. Because of my recent experience with the boards exam, I was feeling pretty down. I was getting disappointed about my lack of continued improvement. It was not only affecting my ability to function at a high level as a doctor, but was also affecting my ability to be the kind of husband and father I wanted and expected myself to be. I wasn't happy with my social skills either and felt I had alienated myself from many important people in my life.

I still trusted that God was in control, but I really didn't approve of his plan at the time. I wanted to be back in control again (*like I ever really was!*). It was then that I heard one of the speakers at the conference say something that changed me, or at the very least it started the process of my true transformation. I don't recall who the speaker was or his topic, but he quoted a verse from Revelations. It was a verse I was familiar with, but one that I had never looked at the way I did that day.

> *I know your deeds, that you are neither cold nor hot. I wish you were either one or the other! So, because you are lukewarm—neither hot nor cold—I am about to spit you out of my mouth. (Rev. 3:15–16, NIV)*

When I heard that verse in the past, I would just feel sorry for the ones getting "spit out" because they had no idea what was coming. This time when I heard it, I saw myself as one of them. I had been living my faith life "lukewarm" and didn't see anything wrong with it. I was so concerned about what other people would say if I went over the top and started taking *all* of God's commandments seriously, so I never got too serious about my faith. After this awakening, my heart changed and I would never be the same. I didn't change into some spiritual super hero all at once. But I started the process of being transformed into what God wanted me to be, and it was this verse that opened my eyes and changed my heart.

I became hungry for anything related to Jesus and the gospel. I started reading books on Christian living, reading blogs, watching videos on RightNow Media, reading, and actually studying and applying truths in the Bible. God spoke to me through that message, and I realized that in order to truly encounter my new normal, I had to start living a true Christian life. This changed how I lived my life, how I worked, how I treated others, how I viewed others. I wish this had happened all at once, but that's not how God works. He is molding us into what he wants us to be. We just have to be willing to be used for him in whatever way he sees fit.

I started to see this theme of Jesus's dislike of "lukewarmness" throughout the Bible. I saw Jesus calling out the Pharisees for being lukewarm:

> *What sorrow awaits you teachers of religious law and you Pharisees. Hypocrites! For you are so careful to clean the outside of the cup and the dish, but inside you are filthy—full of greed and self-indulgence! (Matt. 23:25, NLT)*

I didn't just want to clean the outside of my life anymore. I wanted the love of Jesus to encounter every part of my being, so much so that I was content with whatever life would throw at me, no matter how easy or how hard. I didn't want to be lukewarm anymore, I wanted to find my new purpose.. I knew that in order to truly discover the new me, I had to let go of everything I thought belonged to me and fully grab hold of Jesus.

Sharing the Good News

I began to realize that my relationship with God was never intended to be surface level, or even private, but instead it was supposed to be constantly living and public for all the world around me to see. One passage that I frequently refer to regarding the call to a life of public faith is Matthew 5:14–16 (NLT): *"You are the light of the world—like a city on a hilltop that cannot be hidden. No one lights a lamp and then puts it under a basket. Instead, a lamp is placed on a stand, where it gives light to everyone in the house. In the same way, let your good deeds shine out for all to see so that everyone will praise your heavenly Father."*

The core message in these verses is quite clear: just as one wouldn't light a lamp and then cover it to dilute its purpose, a Christian shouldn't discover the hope of Jesus and never share it or keep it hidden from the public eye. The life and deeds of a Christ-follower should exude out of you. For this not to occur would completely contradict the Great Commission: *"to make disciples of all nations, baptizing them in the name of the Father, Son, and Holy Spirit."* (Matt. 28:19, NLT)

It just doesn't make any sense to stay quiet in a world that parades darkness and deceit. Our faith was made to be public. To be shared. To be discussed to those we meet. So what does this mean? It means that you're called to be a shining example of a Christ-follower in all that you do, no matter what you do, no matter where you are, no matter who you meet. I guess I just have a hard time grasping the idea that someone can be fully devoted to Christ yet hide such faith. I understand strategic evangelism as it pertains to countries where Christianity is illegal, but we as Americans have no excuse to be silent when it comes to the existence of our relationships with God. I'm not saying you need to be on the street corner with a banner that says, "I Love Jesus!" But I am saying you should have no issue letting people know who you've given your life to.

> *For I am not ashamed of this Good News about Christ. It is the power of God at work, saving everyone who believes—the Jew first and also the Gentile." (Rom. 1:16, NLT)*

When our lives get caught up in the beauty of the gospel, we realize our existence is no longer about us but instead the many facets that make up the person of Christ. Our vocations as Christ-followers is to share the gospel, the alluring and jaw-dropping beauty of the gospel. Let your faith be known and your faith be strong. Don't keep your relationship with God private, but instead be outspoken and grace-filled.

Finding a Purpose to My Pain

Despite my new heart—this new purpose and passion for Jesus—I continued to ask, "If God wanted to use me, especially as a doctor, why wouldn't he want my brain to be working at full capacity?" Isn't that how I could best be used as a medical provider? I had heard of people being led to the perfect verse at the perfect time. Well, that had never happened to me before, because I am not so sure I had ever tried that hard to do it. But it did one night as I lay awake struggling with this very question.

Because of the extravagance of those revelations, and so I wouldn't get a big head, I was given the gift of a handicap to keep me in constant touch with my limitations. Satan's angel did his best to get me down; what he in fact did was push me to my knees. No danger then of walking around high and mighty! At first I didn't think of it as a gift, and begged God to remove it. Three times I did that, and then he told me,

My grace is enough; it's all you need.

My strength comes into its own in your weakness.

Once I heard that, I was glad to let it happen. I quit focusing on the handicap and began appreciating the gift. It was a case of Christ's strength moving in on my weakness. Now I take in stride and with good cheer these limitations that cut me down to size— abuse, accidents, opposition, bad breaks. I just let Christ take over! And so the weaker I get, the stronger I become. (2 Corinthians 12:7–10, MSG)

I felt as if I'd found the answer. There's no question God could have given me a full recovery, and that would be another testimony I could share. But that was not his choice. His plan was to give me another "gift," the gift of a TBI. That way I could always remember where my power comes from and that it wasn't from anything of my own doing.

Craig Groeschel said, *"We might impress people with our strengths, but we connect with people through our weaknesses."*[6] God had given me this weakness so I could help others dealing with similar situations and to point them towards my source of strength. Man, I wish I always had this positive and upbeat mindset, but I don't. That is why I must remain engaged with people who can remind me of how far I have come and help me remember that I'm not done yet.

> *Dear TBI,*
> *I never wanted you in my life and still wish you weren't here, so I know that what I am about to say is going to sound crazy to you. I know I never thought I would say words such as this. But I am starting to think that your presence may have actually helped change my life for the better.*
> *You see, before I met you, I really thought I was something. I felt I had a good handle on my life and could deal with most things on my own. After you showed up, it was a much different story. I couldn't do it all by myself anymore, so I had to start getting help from friends, family, doctors, and therapists. But most importantly, it wasn't until after we met that I finally understood my need for Jesus. I started to see Jesus for who he*

---

6   Craig Groeschel (@craiggroeschel), "We might impress people with our strengths, but we connect with people through our weaknesses," Twitter, September 3, 2013, 10:34 a.m., https://twitter.com/craiggroeschel/status/374918426327650304.

is and how small and powerless I was in relation
to him and without him. Before you came, I had
been so busy trying to please God and earn my
salvation with all my "good" behavior. Now I
know that I can never do enough, but that Jesus
has already done it for me. He is all I need.
And when I finally stopped trying to do it on
my own, I started finding true joy, peace, and
contentment. So yes, TBI, you may have changed
me, but Jesus changed me more than you ever will.
—JEFF

CHAPTER 6

The New Normal

Dear TBI,
I wish there could have been another way, and
I am sure that God didn't want this to happen.
He never wanted to send his only son to die on
a cross for our sins, but just like it was with the
cross, maybe he sent you here because you were
the only way for me to find and meet the real
Jesus. I can't believe I am saying this to you,
TBI, but if that's the case, I am actually thankful
you came into my life!
—JEFF

I have told you these things, so that in me you
may have peace. In this world you will have trouble.
But take heart! I have overcome the world. (John
16:33, NIV)

Despite all of my drastic changes and the arrival of my "new normal," I was still somehow able to continue working as a doctor, a miracle in and of itself. I believe that being able to keep practicing medicine was one of the things that kept me focused. It's something I enjoyed doing and I loved helping my patients. It still gave me the sense of worth I needed in life at that time.

But this didn't last. Eventually, because of complications from my traumatic brain injury, I wasn't able to do this anymore. This was when my "new normal" changed even more! It was almost like I now had a "new, new normal." And this happened rather abruptly.

The End of Practicing Medicine

I was finally starting to find myself again. I was settling into my new normal, complete with my new heart. I had accepted my limitations at work. I felt God was working in my life, and I was slowly handing everything over to him. I was always learning things about Jesus that I didn't know before and I was in awe of who he was. I was confident that both my success at work and growth spiritually would continue for many years to come.

It was right after Christmas of 2015; our family decided to take a vacation to Nashville and we were staying at the Opryland Hotel. We didn't say it to each other at the time, but both my wife and I could see us one day coming back and living there. It is hard to explain, but we just had this feeling. However, we both discounted the idea and moved it to the back of our minds for the time being. I was still happily working as a doctor in northwest Indiana. We were part of a great church there. We lived close to many wonderful friends and family, so I assumed we would live there indefinitely. I couldn't see any reason we would ever move away. But we had no idea what was about to happen.

When we returned from our vacation in January of 2016, I got back to working as usual. But this changed rather suddenly when something happened that would once again greatly alter our lives.

Following my head injury, I had started having migraine headaches, and these seemed to be getting worse and more frequent. For the first time, one was so severe I had to go to the ER. While I was there, they performed an MRI on my brain to rule out anything acute or life threatening. I had an appointment with my neurologist for a follow-up a couple days after, and we reviewed my MRI findings. He was able to compare my new MRI with an old one and it showed some findings that concerned him, and me. My brain had a lot of scar tissue from my injury, which I was already aware of, but it showed evidence that my brain was starting to shrink. This part was news to my ears and it didn't sound good! Based on these findings and many other symptoms and issues I was dealing with, my doctor recommended I retire immediately.

Now, from the very beginning of my recovery, I had been told by my doctors that the longevity of my career would most likely be affected by my brain injury. When my accident first happened, they assumed my doctoring years were in the rearview mirror. So the fact that I had returned was an unbelievable blessing. But with the way things were going, I thought I could continue at my reduced workload for years to come. I figured maybe my career would be shortened a couple years, but nothing too extreme. And I thought when my career started coming to an end, it would be a gradual thing. But what happened did so very quickly and very unexpectedly.

To be perfectly honest, I was in a state of shock. I was still trusting God had a plan and was in control, but this was certainly not lining up with what I had in mind. You think I would have learned at this point to stop making plans. But I guess what they say is true. Bad habits are hard to break.

Finding Some Answers

When I couldn't practice medicine any longer, I started asking myself all kinds of questions. I had spent most of my life preparing to be a doctor. Now that this was suddenly not an option, what was I supposed to do for the rest of my life? How would our family earn money? How would I stay busy? How could I deal with telling people I was no longer working when I looked exactly the same? How would it be living in a small town where everyone knows you as the doctor but you aren't anymore? Would I be embarrassed that I couldn't practice medicine? Would my family and friends be embarrassed that I wasn't a doctor anymore? Would people even believe me, or would they think I had just given up?

All of these questions were starting to wreak havoc on my well-being. Many of the former unknowns had been answered; now they were replaced by a whole bunch of new ones. I needed to find something to fill my time and take my mind off these troubling questions. We were extremely blessed during this time because God provided for us financially throughout the whole process and I didn't have to immediately start looking for a new job. But what was I going to do? I needed to start trusting God with the unknowns, which you think would have been easy based on how he had taken care of me and my family over the past few years.

This was when many of the things that I had recently learned about God and Jesus started coming back to the forefront of my mind, and I began to find peace with my current situation. For the last few years I had been reading about the truths of God, Jesus, and what he means to each one of us. Maybe it was time for me to start writing some of my own stuff. So even though I hadn't really written much before and didn't consider myself a writer, I started doing it. I began sharing my heart on paper, a personal journal to help me express what I was learning and feeling.

Not Just for Me

Writing my thoughts and feelings down was therapeutic. It made me feel better about myself and what I was going through. But maybe it was time to share these thoughts and words with other people. Even though my verbal skills were not where I wanted them to be, maybe God could use my written words to help others.

This was when I started entertaining the idea of starting, of all things, a blog. Now the "old" me didn't even know what a blog was, but I had been reading several and was thinking maybe I could start one of own. My blog could tell my story of living with a traumatic brain injury and the role my renewed faith played in my recovery. I could explain the false ideas I had about God in the past and how these didn't change me like they should have. But now that I had tasted and seen who he truly was, and is, change was inevitable. I wanted to encourage the people who would read it that God could do the same thing for all of us. I could be open and honest about my deficits and encourage others to as well.

I spent a lot of time on my blog and worked on it for several months before I finally launched it. I decided to call it *Finding Normal: My Journey to Discovering Purpose*. And just like that, a doctor became a blogger. *(You can check out some of my early blog posts in the "Bonus Chapter" at the end of the book.)*

A New Place for a New Normal

When you are fairly well known in town as one of the main doctors, and then suddenly you aren't one anymore, but you look exactly the same, it makes it hard to live there. It makes it hard to move on. And now instead of being the doctor, I was going to be, of all things, a blogger. This is when I started entertaining the idea of moving to the Nashville area, which was just a fleeting idea the December before, but maybe now there was something to it. We started to pray that

God would give us signs of what to do, knowing that a move would be hard for all of us but confident that if God wanted it, we would find the strength and courage to do it. But other than the general feeling we had before, we never had any real reason to make the move.

As I got closer to launching my blog, I started to question my ability to do it. It was so unlike what I had previously done and, to be honest, it was embarrassing to tell people what I planned on doing. I had many questions about how to even do it. I had the material to share, but I wasn't sure how to go about sharing it. On a whim, I reached out to an author and blogger I followed on Twitter, in the small chance that he would give me some guidance. And much to my surprise, he actually did! I soon found out he lived in Franklin, Tennessee, a town just south of Nashville. So maybe this was God giving us a sign.

We continued to pray and spoke to our pastor about our idea of moving and he suggested we take a vacation to Franklin for a couple weeks so our family could see what it would be like to live there and how we could possibly be used down there. We didn't want to be moving just to run away *from* something, we wanted to be running *to* something. We went down to visit right before school started in the summer of 2016 and felt a real peace about the city. We felt like we belonged. We felt like we were home even though we didn't live there. I cannot begin to explain why we felt this way other than it must have been God, so we decided to act upon those feelings. We met the blogger and his family who had helped me set up my blog. He kept encouraging me in my journey of writing and speaking. The more we spent time in Franklin, the more we began to feel God was in this, and it wasn't just our idea or selfish motives. We were looking for our fresh start, and we believed this was the city where we were to do it. We looked at houses while we were down there, and right before we left we made an offer on the home we currently live in. It was just the right thing to do, and we really felt like God had his hand in it.

Since we have moved, I have signed a book deal *(you are reading the book right now!),* shared my story at a few local churches, and I have gotten the opportunity to speak about brain injury to a group of physicians at a hospital. I am not a gifted speaker by any means, but I am hoping to get more experience with this and improve. We are starting to develop relationships with people down here, but know that takes time. We have joined a local church body we love. I know it is hard to say what the future holds, but I certainly know who holds the future. God has taken my crazy story, redeemed all the brokenness and pain, and given it a purpose instead of letting it lay dormant and stale.

God specializes in using the testimonies of others for his glory, and I hope to be a shining example of that. It would be easy for me to say that I wish my accident never happened, but that's the easy way out. Maybe my accident brought me into a season of life that I needed in order for my soul to experience what it means to have a real relationship with God.

I could probably sit here and think about the what-ifs for hours, but the reality is it's not going to help my current situation. What happened to me isn't going to change and, instead, I need to take the tragedy at hand and realize how God is using it. He took my tragedy and turned it into my testimony. He took my mess and turned it into my message. He took my pain and turned it into a new way to see my purpose in life. God has done all of this by redeeming what happened to me. Nothing is wasted with God, and I've learned this first-hand.

Letting Jesus Define My Normal

I've finally realized the only normal worth finding is normal as Jesus defines it. Even though this won't always be the easiest or most popular thing to do, it is always worth it. Once you find that normal, there is no going back to how you were before. In this sense, it mirrors my brain injury. It was impossible to go back to who I was before my brain injury, just as it is impossible to go back to who I was before God changed my heart and changed my normal.

Please don't get me wrong. There are times when my old heart tries to reappear and my old normal starts coming back. An old normal that was characterized by misplaced priorities, a lukewarm faith, pride disguised as humility, selfishness disguised as generosity, a half-hearted devotion to God's commandments, and a misguided attempt at following Jesus. When I start going back to this, I soon figure out I don't even want it anymore.

I don't think I will ever find Jesus's kind of normal completely, but that is my desire, and I want to keep getting closer. And I want to help people know they can too. This "new normal" is something I learn more about each day, but I'll always be doing that. There is no going back to how I used to be—my old normal—no matter how hard I try. God is showing me a greater way to live. He is showing me something I had missed for many years of being a Christian. And instead of normal, God is showing me purpose, the same purpose God has for anyone who calls themselves a Christian: to love him and love the people he made.

Abnormal Found

abnormal: deviating from what is normal or usual.

In regard to my Christian faith, I always made sure to stay as "normal" as possible. I was careful not to stand out too much from the crowd. I didn't want to go overboard when it came to anything Jesus related. My focus on maintaining normalcy led to me becoming lukewarm, which I have since discovered is something that Jesus despises (see Rev. 3:16). And here's the scary thing. I wasn't even aware of it. I was awakened to my own "lukewarmness," and after being awakened, I started a faith journey that I am still on to this day.

I have learned and am still learning that, when compared to the world's definition of "normal," Jesus desires for us to be the opposite. We should be, and will be, considered strange, different, weird, quirky, peculiar (1 Pet. 2:9).

So when it comes to being a Christian, I no longer want to considered "normal." My new desire is to be "abnormal."

An Unknown Future

Based on the nature of my brain injury, my future prognosis is unpredictable. My current health status is far better than any of my doctors ever thought and any of my current brain-imaging studies predict. This could continue indefinitely, but it could also decline, and I want to be prepared for that if it happens. My memory is the one thing I am most nervous about, and I felt the need to write my entire story down in case one day I forget what happened. This is one of the many reasons I started my blog and wrote this book. I don't know how much longer I will be able to share my story. I don't know how much longer I will be able to share the hope of Jesus with others and tell others of what he has done for me and what he wants to do for all of us. That's why I couldn't put it off any longer.

Although I will never be able to practice medicine again, I've found a new love for writing, speaking, and helping other families who have been affected by brain injury and other life-changing experiences. I want other people who are going through trials and hardships to know that hope is available, and although life will never be the same, it can still be vibrant and fulfilling.

One of the lessons I am taking from this, and it sounds cliché, is that life is short. I mentioned that my future is unclear because of my brain injury, but that was even true before. It is true for all of us. While we are here on earth, let's live everyday like it's our last day. Let's learn from the past, but not live in it. Let's prepare for the future, but let's live in the present! Let's remember why we are here and who we belong to!

*****

We all have difficulties. Some are big. Some are small. Some are self-inflicted. Some are caused by others. Some are common. Some are unique. And because of that, whether we know it or not, we all have a story to tell. I have hesitated to share my story up to this point. I believe that is mainly because of embarrassment. Not embarrassment over the deficits from my traumatic brain injury, but over the fact that it took a brain injury for me to recognize so many amazing truths about God, Jesus, and the Holy Spirit, to learn that even before my brain injury, I already had a story to tell.

I wrote this book for a few reasons: to tell people my story and how God saved my life and changed my heart, to encourage others, to tell them that God has a plan for them no matter what they have experienced in life, and to help others know that there is no tragedy too big for God. I want my kids to see that their dad never gave up when things got tough, but he also didn't try to act like everything was perfect. I'm okay admitting my faults, my flaws, my brokenness, and my doubts. Only when we learn to admit these things can we truly find healing; healing that only can come from Jesus.

Here I am, a doctor who lost his ability to practice medicine, almost died from a car accident, and suffered a severe TBI. Was it easy? Not even close. Is it over? Never. This journey is ongoing, but I know that God will be with me the entire way, guiding me, directing me, keeping me safe, and offering his hand of grace to my life.

I truly hope you understand the main point of my story isn't me. It isn't even my brain injury. I hope you see the main point of my story is Jesus, how much he loves us and what he wants to do in you and for you, no matter what you may be facing. Jesus is there for you every step of the way.

*****

When I stop and think about all that has taken place over the last five years, I believe more than ever that even when it doesn't seem like it, God is in control. He can redeem anything. God transforms tragedy into victory, loss into gain. He can take what is unexpected and unplanned and turn it into just what we need.

You intended to harm me, but God intended it for good to accomplish what is now being done, the saving of many lives. (Gen. 50:20, NIV)

Blog Posts from Finding Normal@jeffhuxford.com

When Brain Injury Changed My Mind, God Changed My Heart

A traumatic brain injury literally changed my mind, and this changed many things about me. I had spent the majority of my life acquiring knowledge and skill to achieve what I wanted, and now the very thing I had used to do it—my brain—was injured beyond repair. I worked hard to get it back, but no matter how hard I tried, it wasn't happening the way I thought it should. I became interested in things that, in the past, I thought were weird. There were things I enjoyed from my past that I didn't anymore. Honestly, I was confused by all this. I wasn't even sure who I was. In some ways I liked who I was becoming, but I was concerned what others were going to think. Because I was concerned about the opinions of others, I was hesitant to act upon what my heart was telling me.

This was a difficult time. I felt like I wasn't being true to myself or others, and even more importantly, being untrue to what God desired for me. This was a tiresome and unsustainable way to live. I knew something had to give. So I did what I thought I would never do. I gave up on trying to be who I once was. But when I gave up, God did an amazing thing. He started changing my heart. In ways likened to my changed mind, but more profound, when God changed my heart, everything about me changed. I was motivated by and cared about things that I used to ignore. It was no longer good enough to feel the right feeling. I didn't want to just know the right thing; I wanted to do the right thing.

God changed my heart, so I need not take any credit for it. But I don't think it would have happened if I hadn't given up on who I used to be. When I finally did that and asked God to take over my life, he was right there waiting, and I am becoming who he wanted me to be from the very beginning.

Comfort Should Not Be Our Goal

I grew up with the mindset that "being comfortable" was the goal of life. I wanted to live a life with no worries. If I tried something and felt a little uneasy doing it, then it was time to stop and go back to my comfort zone. I lived this way for many years and still worry that sometimes comfort is my goal. I look at the choices I still make today, the things I do and don't do, and know that comfort is still important to me, or at least way more important than it should be.

Sometimes I am emotionally torn over my new view on comfort. I know that Jesus does not call us to a life of comfort. But since I suffered my brain injury, I know that I have to take care of myself to be able to serve other people. I think sometimes I take this to the extreme, so this is something I need to be aware of at all times. I don't want to use my brain injury as an excuse to live a pampered life. I want to use my brain injury as a way to help other people in whatever way I can.

In the past, comfort always included surrounding myself with people who looked, thought, and acted pretty much the same as me. This was comfortable for me and so that's what I did. I never thought of myself as being judgmental against people who were different from me; I just didn't see any value in hanging out with them. It's different now. Now I see them as creatures of God, and realize I need people different from me in my life so I can understand their perspectives. I don't just want to surround myself with people who believe the same things I do, because I believe diversity strengthens my beliefs and my faith. I know this is something I need to be intentional about.

I know that if I want to get stronger physically, I will have to lift weights. If I want to build stamina and endurance, I will have to run a lot. Both of these things require hard work and will inevitably lead to some discomfort. But both will result in growth. The same holds true with spiritual growth. If we want to grow in our faith and grow closer into what Jesus wants us to be, it will cause us to be uncomfortable. But I am confident that it will be worth it.

I have heard the saying "being comfortable with being uncomfortable," but I want the opposite to be true for me. I want to be "uncomfortable with being comfortable," because if I'm comfortable for too long, that means I've stopped growing.

Idolatry and Me

Most people, especially ones who grew up in the church, are familiar with the Ten Commandments. I always felt I did a superb job of keeping them. There was even one of the ten that I never thought twice about because it wasn't even a temptation of mine.

> *"You shall not make for yourself an idol." (Exod. 20:4, NLT)*

Idolatry is defined as "the worship of idols," which to me meant bowing down to some symbol or statue that represented a false god, and I'd certainly not ever done that. However, when I started reading books on the subject, I decided I should probably take a closer look at my life. Maybe there was more to this commandment on idolatry than I thought. The more I looked into it, the more I learned it wasn't what I thought it was.

There is a second definition for idolatry, which is "extreme admiration, love, or reverence for something or someone." When I read that one, I became highly concerned. I knew then that idolatry is something that tempts us all. I have even heard it said that "idolatry is the root of all sin," and I've come to believe that's true. Any time we make something else more important than the one true God, we become idolaters. I am still an idolater, and I will always be. Although the idols change, they remain. They never leave. I guess the main difference now is I know I have idols, and I try not to judge others because of theirs. I do think the Holy Spirit living in me helps me recognize my idols much sooner.

Some of the many idols in my life included money, comfort, reputation, image, family, and intelligence. I am not saying that all of these are gone and never to return, but I believe my brain injury took away some of the grip they had on my life. I sometimes wonder if my TBI hadn't taken away some of their power, if I would still be regularly bowing to these things. I know God works in mysterious ways, and I just wonder if he killed these idols for me because he knew I couldn't do it by myself. Whatever the case was, God is the one who deserves the credit.

It is beyond my comprehension why God chose to love us knowing how many times we would turn our backs to him. How many times we would knowingly, or unknowingly, choose to make something or someone more important than him. It is a love that knows no limits, a love I will accept, and a love I try to pass on to and share with others, regardless of who they are and what I get in return.

Ten Things I Learned About the One True God After a Traumatic Brain Injury

I need to tell you something before you read these. I don't deserve credit for any of my "post TBI" education!

You see, for all of my life, I used my mind to learn new things. My mind served me quite well during my many years of schooling, which ultimately resulted in a successful career as a family physician. Then, without warning, TBI roared into my life and took away much of my brain power, the power I had counted on for so long.

But my learning was far from over. And for this I am grateful, because there was still so much I needed to be taught. This was only possible because God changed my heart, giving me the ability to learn these things I'm about to share with you.

1. **If I allow him to, God can make me strong in my weakness.** I spent the majority of my life trying to do things by my own power. My brain injury took away much of the power I had depended on for so long. But it was replaced by something much greater: a changed heart powered by the Holy Spirit, which has given me more strength than I could ever gather on my own.

2. **Life is short.** My life changed in an instant, but it could just have easily ended the morning of May 3, 2012. I am learning to treat every day like it's my last.

3. **Actions speak louder than words.** This one is pretty self-explanatory, but I need to make sure what I'm doing matches what I am saying. If it doesn't, then I lose credibility, and my chance of having a positive influence is greatly diminished.

4. **I have learned the power Jesus can have in my life and have come to realize I must share it with others.** I believe that Jesus is my source of strength and purpose in this life, and not just my free ticket out of hell. Out of love, not out of an effort to earn God's favor, I should want to live for him and share with everyone what I believe and why I believe it.

5. **Treat others like people, not projects, and engage with people who are different from you.** As a follower of Jesus, I am called to treat all people with love, kindness, and respect. I am called to display the love of Jesus to everyone in all that I say and do, and leave the heart change up to God. And I am learning it is important to engage and befriend those who look, act, and think differently than me.

6. **I learned to stop asking the question "why me?" and instead started asking "why not me?"** God used my wife Jacqui to teach me this valuable lesson. She developed this mindset early on in my recovery, while I was still laying in the hospital in a near-comatose state. People would tell her they didn't understand why something this bad happened to such "good" people. They said it just didn't make any sense. She would just respond with, "Why not

us?" She understood God was in control and that he could somehow use what we were going through for good. "Why me?" is a question I still wrestle with at times, but I am learning to be confident in the God I serve and that the plans he has for me far exceed any I may have.

7. **God gave me a story and I need to use it to help others.** I used to complain that I didn't have a story to tell, or at least not the kind that would have an impact on others. Looking back, this was faulty thinking, because we all have a story to tell. But after my accident, I could no longer use that as an excuse. God gave me a story and I feel I need to tell it, not with the intentions of bringing attention to myself, but to point to the author of my story.

8. **I am not supposed to do life on my own.** My brain injury was humbling. I could no longer do certain things on my own power. I started using a lot of new tools and tricks (e.g., Apple Watch, schedules, reminders) to help me function in my daily life. I also learned to accept the help of others. But most importantly, I learned to accept God's help, the loving God who had been there all along just waiting for me to give up on doing it myself and simply surrender my life to him.

9. **Don't judge where someone is, because you don't know where they started.** I have learned to pass less judgment on how someone is living their life. This is something that I am still learning and don't always

do. But it's something that's important to remember if I want to understand, relate to, and help others.

10. **It is important to regularly check my list of priorities and make changes when needed.** After my brain injury, this was something I had to do almost immediately, because I could no longer do all the things I used to do. I had to figure out what I could still do, decide what was important, and focus on these. This involved saying "no" to a lot of good things so I could say "yes" to the more important things.

Without a TBI, I may have never stopped relying on my own "brain power," never understood the power of a changed heart, and never learned these invaluable lessons. I am sure you have heard it said that "God works in mysterious ways." Growing up, I know I heard it countless times. It wasn't until my brain injury that I learned the truth behind this statement and the true wonder of how God works.

Learning to Be Honest

After my accident, people would approach me and make the following types of statements:

- Glad you are back to 100 percent!
- Wow, you look normal!
- You'll be back to yourself in no time!

- Based on how your truck looked after your accident, you are one lucky guy!

I totally understood why they were saying these things. Because if you were to just look at or have a casual conversation with me, you would think I was getting along just great. And I also knew the people saying them were just trying to encourage me. But none of these statements were true. The truth was:

- I was not back to 100 percent.
- I didn't feel normal.
- It was highly unlikely that I would ever get back to myself.
- I certainly didn't feel lucky.

Instead of telling them the truth, I would simply say thanks and let them go on thinking I was doing great. But I couldn't get beyond the fact that I was trying to portray a life that wasn't my reality. I read a quote by Craig Groeschel that said, *"We might impress people with our strengths, but we connect with people through our weaknesses."*[7] It resonated with me and gave me the courage to start living differently.

I could no longer go on living as if I was back to "normal." It was tiresome and, for me, proving to be unsustainable and not beneficial for anyone involved. Thus began my journey toward a life of transparency, honesty, and vulnerability.

---

7   Groeschel, https://twitter.com/craiggroeschel/ status/374918426327650304.

Because of my trouble finding the right words to verbalize how I am feeling or what I am thinking, a complication of my traumatic brain injury, this has proven to be challenging. Despite that, I am committed to living this type of life.

We were never designed to do life on our own! I know being open and honest isn't easy and can be very uncomfortable. But we all need people we can fully trust. People who know what is really going on in our lives and how we are really doing.

Changing Relationships

Some brain injuries may cause a person to look different because they walk or talk different, or they may have a scar on their head from a surgery. But many people look exactly the same. That is the case with me. I look no different than I did before. This is something for which I am very grateful.

But there are other times I wish I had something I could show people that would remind them that I have suffered a severe TBI. Not so I could get sympathy, but people would understand me better and wouldn't take things personally when I act differently than I did before. Because, like I have said, I am very different.

Despite my best efforts, I couldn't get back to who I was before. And when I forget that and try anyway, it leads to a lot of frustration and disappointment. Despite not wanting to be affected by other people's expectations, if somebody viewed me as unchanged, I'll naturally try to give them the unchanged me.

I hope this is something I get better at. I know that if I am going to get better I have to surround myself with people who know and understand why I am different. Or at least try to help people understand TBI. I still have some close relationships with people I knew from before my TBI, but I think I have somewhat of a natural tendency to be drawn to new people because they don't have the expectations of how I used to be. With someone who didn't know me before my brain injury, I can go in with a blank canvas and I can be who I am now, with no pressure to be who I was previously.

Before and After

Lastly, here is something I wrote awhile back. Albeit not a blog post, it's a writing where I talk about the dramatic differences between my Before and After and the one responsible for that.

For many years, the phrase "Head knowledge without heart knowledge" characterized my "normal," and I didn't even think it was a problem. Head knowledge may have changed my appearance and what I was doing or not doing, but it didn't change who I was on the inside and the reasons why I was doing what I was doing. I find it a bit ironic that it took a severe injury to my head for these truths to make their way to my heart, but when they did, everything about me changed. This has been the main source of power for my new normal.

This not only fueled my new normal but also changed the whole way I think about normal. Normal, if there even is such a thing, was no longer my goal, at least not the way our culture defines it or the way I defined it before. I needed to redefine normal, and that's what Jesus did for me. But in order to let him do this and show me what normal means to him, I had to first get rid of all of the assumptions that had always shaped my faith and determined my behavior so they could be replaced with real, life-changing truths.

- **Before:** I would talk to and ask God for help, but only after I first tried to do it myself, sometimes multiple times. But I always had Jesus tucked away in my back pocket just in case I really needed him.
  After: Jesus is our first line of defense and offense. I can do nothing without him.

- **Before:** I made sure that I was avoiding all the "bad" things I needed to avoid, but didn't give much thought to what I was actually supposed to do.
  After: I am still trying to avoid the "bad" things, but I am no longer content with that. I want to do the things that God wants me to do. The things Jesus demonstrated for me when he was here on this earth.

- **Before:** I counted on the fact that I always knew the right thing to do but never gave much thought to actually doing it! I believed knowing was enough.

After: Knowing and not doing is the same as not knowing. Faith and knowledge without action is dead!

- **Before:** I based my worthiness or holiness on how I compared to other people. I was confident because knew I was doing better than most. And I was sure God was grading on a curve.

  After: God does not grade on a curve. His only judge for our goodness is Jesus, who was perfect. None of us can meet this standard, but God has given us a way to be seen as worthy by Jesus's sacrifice. If we accept that and live for him, God sees Jesus when he sees us.

- **Before:** I always believed Jesus died for my sins and saved me from hell, but I didn't really understand that I needed him for the strength to live for him in this life.

  After: The power of the cross and Jesus gives us the power to live for him every day. We don't have to wait until we die to see his power, although that is when we will see it unhindered and in full force. But through his power, we can bring a little heaven to earth right now, every day.

- **Before:** I was what Craig Groeschel calls a "Christian Atheist." I believed in God but was living as if he didn't exist, not in any obvious, outward ways, but in the inner workings of my mind, its thoughts, and attitudes.

After: I believe in God and want my actions to show that he's real to me by how I act. It isn't enough to just believe. In fact, I think if we truly believe, our actions will be inevitably affected.

- **Before:** I was following what Mark Batterson calls the "inverted gospel."[8] I stated I was following God but had really just invited him to follow me. And if God was following me, then I had nothing to worry about.

  After: I want to follow God wherever he leads despite my own wishes or preferences, even if that means being uncomfortable.

- **Before:** I had heard of the Holy Spirit and thought of "it" as more of a "guidance counselor" than anything else. The Holy Spirit, which I always knew of as the Holy Ghost, was "something" that could help me make decisions but the power for those decisions depended on me.

  After: The Holy Spirit is real and not just a made-up thing that will help us. He is alive and living inside all of us who believe. He not only guides us, but he powers us.

---

8   Mark Batterson, *All In: You Are One Decision Away from a Totally Different Life* (Zondervan, 2013).

- **Before:** I counted on my good works to prove myself to God. And I was always confident that I was doing enough good to outweigh the bad. And I knew that God used a scale to evaluate my obedience.

  After: I know I could never do enough to outweigh the sin in my life. I still desire to do good works, but not so God will forget about the bad. Because of Jesus, he has already forgotten. I want to do these good works because of what he has done for me.

- **Before:** I didn't see why Jesus needed to be included in all aspects of my life. I would compartmentalize my life and only allow Jesus into the parts where I felt could get something out of him or where I felt he would better my image.

  After: I have let God into every aspect of my life. I am no longer blocking him out of the areas where I would just rather handle things myself. He is welcome everywhere.

- **Before:** I was more concerned with the opinions of others than I was with the opinion of God. I wanted to be a Christian, but I didn't want to be thought of as one of those people who went overboard.

  After: I am all in for Jesus. I wish I could rid myself of not caring about others' opinions, except the people I respect and love, but if I am being honest, I still do. However, I remain confident this is something that will get better.

- **Before:** I knew I was guilty of sin but was also confident that Jesus died for my sins. But my sin never grieved me because I knew many other people doing far worse things than me.

  After: I am starting to view my sin differently. My sin is beginning to grieve me. I don't want to take advantage of God's grace and love, and I am finding this is much harder to do while in a constant relationship with my Savior.

- **Before:** Even when I felt close to God and I was spiritually healthy, I didn't feel it was my duty or that I was qualified to tell others about Jesus and what he has done for me. That was a job for "professional" Christians.

  After: Because of what God has done for me, I can't help but tell people about him. This is somewhat challenging with my speech difficulties, but I am finding a good outlet for this in my blog. I want to get better with my verbal skills and am confident that if God wants this, he will make it happen. I know now that we are all powered by the same Spirit, so we all have the ability to share our faith in our own unique ways, and maybe not in the way we expected.

- **Before:** Small groups were a good addition, but not all that important or necessary.

After: We like to ask ourselves the question WWJD, or What Would Jesus Do? Well, he started his church with a small group.

I am the process of ridding myself of these misconceptions. I reckon this will be a lifelong process. But it is changing me and I am finding that as I continue to replace these falsehoods with real, life-giving truths of Jesus, it leaves me hungry and thirsty for more.

ACKNOWLEDGMENTS

When I set out to write this book, I was getting overwhelmed trying to think of all the people who've played an important role in my life. So, I apologize, but I went the safe route. Instead of trying to list off everyone and, undoubtedly, leaving off several meaningful people, please know that if you have played a significant role in my life, I love and thank each and every one of you from the bottom of my heart, and I know that none of this would be possible without your love and support. When I see you in person, I will be sure to tell you this again! And if I don't, please remind me! Because, as you just read, my memory isn't so good!

Most importantly, I would like to thank my Lord and Savior, Jesus Christ, who has always been with me, giving me strength, guiding and directing me all along the way, even when I wasn't aware of his presence.

Thank you, Jesus, for giving me a story and thank you for saving my life so I could tell it. I hope and pray I tell it well and it points people right back to you.

—JEFF

ABOUT THE AUTHOR

At the beginning of 2016, Jeff Huxford, M.D. had to stop practicing medicine due to complications from a severe traumatic brain injury (TBI) he had sustained in a 2012 near fatal car accident. Prior to that, he was a family doctor in northwest Indiana for ten years.

In the fall of 2016, Jeff, along with his wife (Jacqui) and two children (Jayse, Jenna), moved to Franklin, TN. He is now an author, blogger, and speaker. In his spare time. Jeff enjoys watching both his kids play sports and is an avid reader of nonfiction books.

Jeff can be found on Facebook (www.facebook.com/jeffhuxfordmd), Twitter (@jeffhuxford), and Instagram (jeffhuxford). He also has a blog at jeffhuxford.com.

He can be reached by email at:
newnormal5312@gmail.com

Hope

after brain injury

All net proceeds from the sale of *Finding Normal*
will go to Hope After Brain Injury (HABI)
(HopeAfterBrainInjury.org)

HABI is a faith based non-profit organization
devoted to sharing hope with those affected by
brain injury through counseling, education, and
connection to community resources. We consist
of brain injury survivors with their caregivers
and healthcare professionals committed to the
advancement of brain injury recovery.